Peacock Books
Editor: Kaye Webb
OVERKILL: The Story of Modern Weapons

The splitting of the atom is recognized as one of the major scientific achievements of the twentieth century, but what has it meant for us? So far we have not seen nuclear power harnessed to provide us with cheap and efficient heating and lighting for our homes, or energy to drive our factories and cars. Instead, we have seen two nuclear bombs used in war – together they killed a quarter of a million people. There is now an amazing variety of sophisticated ICBMs, MIRVs, LRCMs and SLBMs which could wipe us off the face of the earth: the threat of nuclear holocaust is ever present.

In *Overkill* Dr John Cox explains for the non-specialist the scientific and historical backgr [illegible] tells the story of the Hiroshim [illegible] to explain nuclear energy and h [illegible] estruction. He describes the curr [illegible] how war might start, tells of in [illegible] r weapons. Finally in a few powe [illegible] argues that only complete disarmament can make the world safe.

With a glossary of strategists' terms, many informative photographs and simple scientific diagrams, and most of all with its widely informed yet clearly written text, *Overkill* offers a fascinating combination of history and science that should appeal to anyone interested in what is happening right now.

Dr John Cox was born in Cardiff in 1935, where he went to school before studying mathematics and chemical engineering at Imperial College, London. He works as a consultant engineer, though much of his spare time is spent lecturing on the dangers of the arms race. He is Chairman of the Campaign for Nuclear Disarmament. Dr Cox is married with two children and lives in Crawley, Sussex.

BOOM!
BLOODY FRENCH!
BB/'89
BOOM!
BLOODY INDIANS!
BOOM!
BLOODY POMS!

John Cox

Overkill

The story of modern weapons

With a preface by Professor Joseph Rotblat

Penguin Books

Penguin Books Ltd,
Harmondsworth, Middlesex, England
Penguin Books, 625 Madison Avenue, New York,
New York 10022, U.S.A.
Penguin Books Australia Ltd,
Ringwood, Victoria, Australia
Penguin Books Canada Ltd,
41 Steelcase Road West, Markham, Ontario, Canada
Penguin Books (N.Z.) Ltd,
182–190 Wairau Road, Auckland 10, New Zealand

First published 1977
Published simultaneously in hardback by Kestrel Books

The diagrams were drawn by R. Sherrington

Filmset by BAS Printers Limited, Wallop, Hampshire
Printed in Great Britain by Fletcher and Son Ltd, Norwich
Set in 'Monophoto' Apollo

Contents

Acknowledgements

The author and publishers would like to thank the following for their kind permission to reproduce extracts from copyright material: pp. 134–5 'New Chips for SALT' by Art Buchwald, from the *International Herald Tribune,* to the author; pp. 22, 24–5 *Nagasaki: The Forgotten Bomb* by F. W. Chinnock, copyright © 1969 by F. W. Chinnock, reprinted by permission of Allen & Unwin Ltd and The New American Library, Inc., New York; pp. 15–20 *Hiroshima Diary* by Michihiko Hachiya, copyright © 1958 by Michihiko Hachiya, reprinted by permission of Gollancz and Collins-Knowlton-Wing; pp. 186–7 'The Dangers of Leaving Defence Planning to "Experts"' by Mary Kaldor, reproduced from *The Times,* 29 October 1975, by permission; pp. 40–43 Frederick Muller Ltd, *The Voyage of the* Lucky Dragon, by Ralph E. Lapp, to the author; pp. 114–15 *The Essence of Security* by Robert S. McNamara, copyright © 1968 by Robert S. McNamara, by permission of Harper & Row, Publishers, Inc.; pp. 164–5 'Warfare is Only an Invention – Not a Biological Necessity' by Margaret Mead, from *Asia,* vol. 40, no. 8, 1940, pp. 402–5, to the author; p. 36 extract from the *Western Daily Press,* 20 July 1974, to the editor.

The author and publishers would like to thank the following for their kind permission to reproduce illustrative material: Associated Press Ltd for pp. 11, 14, 41, 43, 77, 97 and 144: Associated Newspapers Ltd/British Museum Newspaper Library for p. 28; ATOM Committee for pp. 158, 169, 177 and 191; BBC copyright photograph, p. 164; Bill Mauldon/*Chicago Sun Times* for p. 132; *Guardian*/cartoon by Papas for p. 183; HMSO for pp. 108 and 109; The Home Office/COI for pp. 50–51 and 54–5; Imperial War Museum for pp. 18, 21 and 23 *below*; Keystone Press Agency for pp. 17, 39, 42, 46, 61, 66, 67, 79, 82, 84,

114, 119 *both*, 120 *above*, 121 *middle*, 125, 130, 153, 159 and 180; Kyodo Photo Service for p. 44; *Labour Weekly*/cartoon by Murray Ball for title page; Lawrence Radiation Laboratory, Nevada, USA for p. 140; Herb Lock © 1973 for p. 150; Lookout Mountain Air Force Station for p. 49; Ministry of Defence for p. 93; National Film Archives/*Time-Life* for p. 25; *New Statesman*/cartoon by Vicky, 1960 for p. 192; Novosti Press Agency for pp. 110 and 111; Penguin Books Ltd for pp. 59, 171 and 173; Popperfoto for pp. 120 *below*, 121 *below*, 147 and 148; Press Association for p. 104; Pressen Bild Stockholm, Sweden for p. 70; *Punch* for p. 63; RAF photo/DOE © Crown copyright for p. 143; *Sanity* for pp. 117 and 161; *Scientific American* from pp. 18–19 of 'The Great Test Ban Debate' by Herbert F. York, November 1972 issue, for p. 40/from pp. 19–21 of 'Missile Submarines and National Security' by Herbert Scoville Jr, June 1972 issue, for pp. 106 and 107/from p. 29 *top* of 'The Detection of Underground Explosions' by Sir Edward Bullard, July 1966 issue, for p. 141/from p. 15 of 'The Accuracy of Strategic Missiles' by Kosta Tsipis for p. 155; Ullstein Bilderdienst for p. 64; US Air Force Department for pp. 75 and 156; US Defense Nuclear Agency for pp. 13, 23 *above*; US Navy Department for pp. 92, 94, 95 *both*, 122 and 123; Navy Department/National Archives for p. 126; Visnews Ltd for p. 121 *above*; A. H. Westing for pp. 72 *both* and 73; Wylfa Power Station for p. 35.

Preface by Professor Joseph Rotblat

About two thirds of the world population in 1976 were born *after* the bombs on Hiroshima and Nagasaki. For the pre-atomic generation the news in 1945 of the unleashing of a new immensely powerful and awesome source of energy was a tremendous shock. Except for a small number of scientists, nobody suspected its coming, and its demonstration in such a spectacular and tragic manner made 6 August 1945 a turning point in the history of mankind: from then onwards the continued existence of the human species on this planet could no longer be taken for granted.

This cataclysmic perception of nuclear energy appears to be absent among the majority of people alive today. Born in the atomic age and grown up with *the bomb*, they believe that they can live with it, and give as evidence the fact that since Hiroshima and Nagasaki there has been no instance of nuclear weapons being used for military purposes. While everybody agrees that a nuclear war would be an unmitigated catastrophe, the attitude towards it is becoming similar to that of potential natural disasters, earthquakes, tornadoes, and other Acts of God: we know the threats exist, but there is nothing we can do about them.

This fatalistic attitude is, of course, fallacious and unrealistic. Unlike Acts of God, which by definition are unpredictable, the occurrence of a nuclear war is a predictable event; its probability is increasing with time. The so-called nuclear stalemate is not a static phenomenon; it is dynamic, and can only be described as a state of unstable equilibrium with a pre-determined outcome.

If, so far, we have managed to avoid a conflict in which nuclear weapons were used (but threats of its use were made on several occasions) it is because no side has yet reached a position from which it could be sure of winning a war without incurring unacceptable damage itself. But they keep trying. This is the essence of the nuclear arms race which goes on unabated and is accelerating in two dimensions: vertically and horizontally.

The vertical arms race, in which the main contestants – at the moment – are the USA and USSR, is the continuous attempt to gain numerical and technological superiority – more, faster, bigger and deadlier missiles; eventually this is bound to result in one side acquiring a first-strike capability. Already it has led to the mad state of affairs, known as overkill, in which the stockpiles of nuclear weapons are considerably more than enough to destroy every human being on the earth.

Perhaps even more dangerous is the horizontal arms race, in which more and more nations acquire the potential to produce nuclear weapons, or to procure them otherwise. The more nations 'go nuclear', the greater is the probability that these will include states with unstable governments or irresponsible leaders, who will not exercise the restraints so far shown by the nuclear powers. There are enough examples of such states at the present time to make this a most terrifying prospect.

If, at one time, it was perhaps conceivable to look at the nuclear arms race as a duel between the USA and USSR, from which other nations, particularly the large number of developing countries, could stay away, this is no longer the case. Nuclear power states now comprise more than half the world's population, and – unless drastic steps are taken – one can predict with certainty that the 'disease of nuclear armaments' will soon spread to the rest of the world. We are in a vicious circle. Many nations will not sign the Non-Proliferation Treaty as long as the nuclear powers do not fulfil their undertaking to implement effective disarmament measures. On the other hand, the USA and the USSR cannot stop the arms race, not only because they do not trust each other, but because they are beginning to feel threatened by the nuclear potential of other nations.

There appears to be only one way out: complete disarmament. All attempts at partial arms control measures – the step-by-step approach which has been tried over the past years – have failed. Our only hope of survival is a return to the earlier concept of bringing the arms race to an end, namely by general and complete disarmament. The arguments leading to this conclusion are lucidly and logically developed by Dr Cox. I hope that the book will be read and debated in many circles, particularly by the young generation.

Joseph Rotblat *Professor of Physics in the University of London at*
May 1976 *St Bartholomew's Hospital Medical College*

Murder: to kill unlawfully with malice aforethought

'Thou shalt not kill'

War: hostilities conducted by organized and premeditated force

'The world is wet with mutual bloodshed and homicide is a crime when individuals commit it but a virtue when many commit it. Not the reason of innocence but the magnitude of savagery assures impunity for crimes' (St Cyprian, 2nd Century AD)

Genocide: extermination of an entire population

The German Nazi leaders 'determined upon and carried out ruthless wars against countries and populations, in violation of the rules and customs of war, including . . . the indiscriminate destruction of cities, towns and villages, and devastation not justified by military necessity' (Nuremberg War Crimes tribunal, 1946)

Overkill: the ability to exterminate a population more than once

'Both the US and the Soviet Union now possess nuclear stockpiles large enough to exterminate mankind three or four – some say ten – times over' (Philip Noel-Baker, Nobel Peace Prize winner, 1971)

Strategic superiority: more overkill than the opponent

'One of the questions we have to ask ourselves as a country is what in the name of God is strategic superiority? What do you do with it?' (Henry Kissinger, US Secretary of State, 1975)

1. The first atomic bombs

In some sort of crude sense which no vulgarity, no humor, no overstatement can quite extinguish, the physicists have known sin; and this is a knowledge which they cannot lose.

J. Robert Oppenheimer,
Director of the first A-bomb project

Atomic weapons were born from the fear that Hitler's Germany would dominate the world with a monopoly of atomic bombs. The initiative for their development came from Dr Leo Szilard, a Hungarian-born refugee from fascism, who obtained the support of Albert Einstein. Einstein, a German-born Jew and a life-long opponent of German militarism, was then living in self-imposed exile in the United States of America. On 2 August 1939 he wrote to the President, Franklin D. Roosevelt, warning of the danger that Germany might develop the bomb:

Some recent work by E. Fermi and L. Szilard, which has been communicated to me in manuscript, leads me to expect that the element uranium may be turned into a new and important source of energy in the immediate future. Certain aspects of the situation seem to call for watchfulness and, if necessary, quick action on the part of the administration. I believe therefore that it is my duty to bring to your attention . . . that extremely powerful bombs of a new type may . . . be constructed. I understand that Germany has actually stopped the sale of uranium from the Czechoslovakian mines which she has taken over . . .

The U S A was not at that time at war and so Einstein's warning did not meet with an energetic response. On 7 March 1940 Einstein, again after an approach from Szilard, wrote a second and more urgent appeal. Preliminary work on bomb manufacture then started, shortly after this second appeal, and by the time they joined the war, U S government and military officials knew that 'extremely powerful bombs of a new type' could be constructed in the way suggested by Szilard and Fermi. In fact the decision to go ahead and build an A-bomb was taken on 6 December 1941 – the day before the Japanese attack on Pearl Harbor which brought America into the war.

In the next four years the scientists worked feverishly to develop atomic weapons in advance of Germany. Enrico Fermi, Leo Szilard, Niels Bohr, Hans Bethe and Joseph Rotblat were among the many Europeans who worked for the project (despite the fact that some were not even American citizens). Several British nuclear scientists also participated. All were united in their fear of what might happen if Hitler were to get the atomic bomb first.

But by November 1944 it was clear that Germany was not in fact making such a bomb. In December 1944 Rotblat, who later became Professor of Physics at St Bartholomew's Hospital Medical College, London, left the project because it no longer seemed necessary. In the spring of 1945 Szilard and Einstein again wrote to Roosevelt, this time with a quite different purpose: to warn him of the dangers which would face the post-war world from the development of atomic energy.

Then, on 8 May 1945, the European war ended and it was confirmed that Germany had never seriously considered building an atomic bomb. The $2,000 million project need never have begun. And there no longer seemed any need to continue with it, since it was known that the Japanese, who were still fighting, had no uranium. At this time the scientists had not got as far as building even a prototype bomb.

Already the more far-seeing were becoming concerned about the long-term implications of atomic weapons. Einstein, Szilard and Bohr had all attempted in different ways to warn the politicians of the coming dangers. They felt that the bomb project could be abandoned and the emphasis switched to peaceful uses of nuclear energy.

After 8 May this feeling began to be shared by more and more of those who had worked to build the bomb. A poll of these atomic scientists was taken and only 15 per cent whole-heartedly favoured its military use against Japan.

Nonetheless, work on the bomb continued with renewed urgency.

Alamogordo

The first atomic test was at Alamogordo in the New Mexico desert on 16 July 1945. According to one eye-witness from more than five miles away:

Alamogordo: the first atomic explosion, 16 July 1945

The whole country was lighted by a searing light with an intensity many times that of the midday sun . . . Thirty seconds after the explosion came, first, the air blast pressing against the people and things, to be followed almost immediately by the strong, sustained, awesome roar which warned of doomsday and made us feel that we puny things were blasphemous to dare tamper with the forces heretofore reserved to the Almighty. Words are inadequate tools for the job of acquainting those not present with the physical, mental and psychological effects. It had to be witnessed to be realized.

Immediately following this test, many atomic scientists signed a petition – drafted by Szilard – urging that the bomb should not be used against Japan without prior demonstration and the opportunity to surrender. It also urged that the American government start immediately to study the possibility of securing international control of the new weapon. The official response to the petition was to declare its contents secret and it was not made public until after the end of the war.

*General Leslie R. Groves (*right*) and Dr J. R. Oppenheimer looking over the remains of a tower from which the test bomb was exploded*

Already there were differences between the United States and Britain on the one hand and their communist ally. The Soviet Union was about to join the war against Japan and the Allies feared that she might occupy Japan whilst American forces were still hundreds of miles away. Though the new weapon was mentioned casually to the Soviet leader Stalin, its full significance was not indicated. The true nature of the Alamogordo test was kept secret whilst preparations went forward to drop the bomb on the Japanese city of Hiroshima.

An Hiroshima Diary*

6 August 1945

The hour was early; the morning still, warm and beautiful. Shimmering leaves, reflecting sunlight from a cloudless sky, made a pleasant contrast with shadows in my garden as I gazed absently through wide-flung doors opening to the south.

Clad in vest and pants, I was sprawled on the living-room floor exhausted because I had just spent a sleepless night on duty as an air-raid warden in my hospital.

Suddenly, a strong flash of light startled me – and then another. So well does one recall little things that I remember vividly how a stone lantern in the garden became brilliantly lit and I debated whether this light was caused by a magnesium flare or sparks from a passing train.

Garden shadows disappeared. The view where a moment before all had been so bright and sunny was now dark and hazy. Through swirling dust I could barely discern a wooden column that had supported one corner of my house. It was leaning crazily and the roof sagged dangerously.

Moving instinctively, I tried to escape, but rubble and fallen timbers barred the way. By picking my way cautiously I managed to reach the roka and stepped down into my garden. A profound weakness overcame me, so I stopped to regain my strength. To my surprise I discovered that I was completely naked. How odd. Where were my vest and pants?

What had happened?

All over the right side of my body I was cut and bleeding. A large

*From *Hiroshima Diary* by Michihiko Hachiya, Gollancz, 1955.

splinter was protruding from a mangled wound in my thigh, and something warm trickled into my mouth. My cheek was torn, I discovered, as I felt it gingerly, with the lower lip laid wide open. Embedded in my neck was a sizeable fragment of glass which I matter-of-factly dislodged, and with the detachment of one stunned and shocked I studied it and my blood-stained hand . . .

'We'll be all right,' I [told my wife.] 'Only let's get out of here as fast as we can.'

She nodded, and I motioned for her to follow me.

The shortest path to the street lay through the house next door so through the house we went—running, stumbling, falling, and then running again until in the headlong flight we tripped over something and fell sprawling into the street. Getting to my feet, I discovered that I had tripped over a man's head.

'Excuse me! Excuse me, please!' I cried hysterically.

There was no answer. The man was dead. The head had belonged to a young officer whose body was crushed beneath a massive gate . . .

We stood in the street, uncertain and afraid, until a house across from us began to sway, and in a minute it, too, collapsed in a cloud of dust. Other buildings caved in or toppled. Fires sprang up and whipped by a vicious wind began to spread . . .

7 August 1945

I must have slept soundly because when I opened my eyes a piercing hot sun was shining in on me. There were no shutters or curtains to lessen the glare – and for that matter no windows . . .

In the space of one night patients had become packed, like the rice in sushi, into every nook and cranny of the hospital. The majority were badly burned, a few severely injured. All were critically ill . . . They came as an avalanche and overran the hospital . . .

Mr Katsutani . . . had come all the way from Jigozen to look for me, and now that he had found me, emotion overcame him.

He turned to Dr Sasada and said brokenly: 'Yesterday, it was impossible to enter Hiroshima, else I would have come. Even today fires are still burning in some places. You should see how the city has changed. When I reached the Misasa Bridge this morning, everything before me was gone, even the castle. These buildings here are the only

Hiroshima: the first A-Bomb target, 6 August 1945

ones left anywhere around. The Communications Bureau seemed to loom right in front of me long before I got anywhere near here.'

Mr Katsutani paused for a moment to catch his breath and went on: 'I *really* walked along the railway tracks to get here, but even they were littered with electric wires and broken railway cars, and the dead and wounded lay everywhere. When I reached the bridge, I saw a dreadful thing. It was unbelievable. There was a man, stone dead, sitting on his bicycle as it leaned against the bridge railing. It is hard to believe that such a thing could happen!'

He repeated himself two or three times as if to convince himself that what he said was true and then continued: 'It seems that most of the dead people were either on the bridge or beneath it. You could tell that many had gone down to the river to get a drink of water and had died where they lay. I saw a few live people still in the water, knocking against the dead as they floated down the river. There must have been hundreds and thousands who fled to the river to escape the fire and then drowned . . .'

8 August 1945

During the day, an effort was made to sort and rearrange the patients according to the nature and severity of their injuries, and not a few dead were found among the living, though fewer than yesterday . . . I felt that the dead should be moved with greater dispatch in order to make room for the living. This is another example of my changed outlook. People were dying so fast that I had begun to accept death as a matter of course and ceased to respect its awfulness. I considered a family lucky if it had not lost more than two of its members. How could I hold my head up among the citizens of Hiroshima with thoughts like that in my mind? . . .

Yaeko-san and I found beds near each other that were not too badly bent. Our sleeping mats were placed over the frames, and without further ado we were ready to resume life in our new quarters . . .

In all four walls were large casement windows which afforded a commanding view in every direction. There were no shutters, no curtains, nor even glass to impose the least obstruction to air or light. Looking east, south and west was an unobstructed view of Hiroshima, and in Hiroshima Bay we could see the island Ninoshima.

Near the centre of the city, some 1,500 metres distant, one could see the blackened ruins of the two largest buildings in Hiroshima, the Fukuya Department Store and the Chugoku Press Building. Hijiyama, the sacred and beautiful little mountain in the eastern sector of the city, looked almost close enough to touch. To our north no buildings remained.

The 'Little Boy' bomb used at Hiroshima weighed 4–5 tons and was 10 feet long with a diameter of 28 inches. Its explosive power was equivalent to about 20,000 tons of conventional explosives

For the first time, I could understand what my friends had meant when they said Hiroshima was destroyed. Nothing remained except a few buildings of reinforced concrete . . . For acres and acres the city was like a desert except for scattered piles of brick and roof tile. I had to revise my meaning of the word destruction or choose some other word to describe what I saw. Devastation may be a better word, but really I knew of no word or words to describe the view from my twisted iron bed in the fire-gutted ward of the Communications Hospital . . .

Towards evening, a light, southerly wind blowing across the city wafted to us an odour suggestive of burning sardines. I wondered what could cause such a smell until somebody, noticing it too, informed me that sanitation teams were cremating the remains of people who had been killed. Looking out, I could discern numerous fires scattered about the city. Previously I had assumed the fires were caused by burning rubble. Towards Nigitsu was an especially large fire where the dead were being burned by hundreds. Suddenly to realize that these fires were funeral pyres made me shudder, and I became a little nauseated.

9 August 1945

Now, I could state positively that I heard nothing like an explosion when we were bombed the other morning, nor did I remember any sound during my walk to the hospital as houses collapsed around me. It was as though I walked through a gloomy, silent motion picture. Others whom I questioned had had the same experience.

Those who experienced the bombing from the outskirts of the city characterized it by the word: *pikadon* . . .*

While I lay there brooding . . . old Mrs Saeki came up quickly and stood by my bed. One look into her pale, careworn face and I knew what she had come to say. Her son was dead; her eldest son – her only child

* *Pika* means a glitter, sparkle or bright flash of light, like a flash of lightning. *Don* means a boom or loud sound. Together, the words came to mean to the people of Hiroshima an explosion characterized by a flash and a boom. Hence 'flash-boom'. Those who remember the flash only speak of the *pika*; those who were far enough from the hypocentre to experience both speak of the *pikadon*. Another word less frequently used in Hiroshima, but no less expressive, is *gembaku*, which literally means 'the place of suffering'.

left in the world. She had been so hopeful yesterday when he was brought in, and now he was gone. Her son's wife and her second son had been killed on the day of the *pikadon*, and now no one was left. She put her hands over her eyes and cried, but her sobs were scarcely audible. I could not speak for a while because there was something in my throat . . .

Darkness came and still there were no lights except the lights from the fires where the dead were burned. And again, the smell of burning flesh. The hospital was quieter, but in the isolation ward, the stillness of the night was broken again and again by the little girl.

At least 75,000 people lost their lives at Hiroshima in the first hours after the bomb was dropped. Most were disintegrated immediately by the fireball; the others died shortly afterwards from burns, blast and shock. The eventual death toll was probably 200,000.

According to the American government, the bomb was used so that the war would end quickly and save lives. Yet the US military command saw no need for the attack. After the event the US Strategic Bombing Survey came to the following conclusion:

It seems clear that, even without the atomic bomb attacks, air supremacy over Japan could have exerted sufficient pressure to bring unconditional surrender and obviate the need for invasion . . . Based on a detailed investigation of all the facts and supported by the testimony of the surviving Japanese leaders involved, it is the survey's opinion that certainly prior to 31 December 1945, Japan would have surrendered even if the atomic bombs had not been dropped, even if Russia* had not entered the war, and even if no invasion had been planned or contemplated.

*Russia is in fact only one of fifteen republics that together make up the Union of Soviet Socialist Republics (USSR) – the 'Soviet Union' – but many people, especially those who remember the old Tsarist Russian Empire, still refer to the Soviet Union as Russia. These terms are used interchangeably throughout the book. Similarly, the USA, though only a part of the American continent, is referred to as 'America' in accordance with common usage.

Eisenhower in 1945

Supreme Commander Eisenhower declared more succinctly, 'It wasn't necessary to hit them with that awful thing.'

If the intention was to save lives, a few days grace would have been appropriate before dropping a second bomb. Communications with Tokyo were so disrupted that it took over a week for the Japanese government to appreciate the strength of the new weapons.

But the politicians were anxious, since Russia had now entered the war. The Russians had originally agreed with the Allies to attack Japan three months after the ending of the war in Europe. Since Germany had surrendered on 8 May, the deadline for Russia's entry into the Japanese war was 8 August – only two days after the bomb was dropped on Hiroshima. There was therefore little time to ensure that Japan would be occupied by America rather than Russia.

So the third atomic bomb was dropped on Nagasaki – on 9 August – even as Dr Hachiya continued to puzzle over the Hiroshima *pikadon*.

Nagasaki

There is a spot in the upper Urakami river where nature has formed a small pool. That morning a group of ten boys, in coloured loincloths, was playing a game called 'find the bell'. One of the boys, eleven-year-old Koichi Nakajima, had a little gilded bell. He would throw it in the water, count to three and they would all dive after it. The first to find it won the game.

Now Koichi held up the tiny bell and shouted, 'Here we go. One, two, three.' There were ten splashes as the boys dived for the prize. But the river had become oily, and no one found it.

Koichi began to get worried. He had taken the bell from his sister's workbox without her permission. She would be very angry if he lost it. He surfaced, took a deep breath, and eeled his way down to the bottom.

Nine seconds later, the bomb exploded over his head. When Koichi surfaced, he heard two of the boys screaming with pain. He stared around in fright. There were bodies of his friends on the riverbank, and beyond them he saw that all the houses had been knocked down. What had been a beautiful city a moment before was now a wasteland with a big, black cloud rising above it like smoke from a funeral pyre. Though it was deadly hot, Koichi's teeth began to chatter.*

When the bomb exploded, heat, light, gamma radiation and pressure were all released, burning many people beyond recognition and simply obliterating others. Hundreds received mass cremation and others died unrecorded after fleeing to the country and mountains. The exact number killed at Nagasaki, like Hiroshima, will never be known, but there were certainly more than 40,000 deaths in the first few seconds.

For three fifths of a mile nearly all unprotected living organisms – birds, insects, horses, cats, chickens – perished instantly. Flowers, trees and plants all shrivelled and died. Wood burst into flames. Metal beams and galvanized iron roofs began to bubble, and the soft gooey masses twisted into grotesque shapes. People within that doomed section neither knew nor felt anything.

*From *Nagasaki: The Forgotten Bomb* by F.W.Chinnock, Allen & Unwin, 1970.

Nagasaki: the second A-bomb target, 9 August 1945

Near the explosion centre (picture first released December 1975)

About half a mile away and screened from damage by the surrounding hills

Fewer were killed instantly at Nagasaki than at Hiroshima because the explosion took place within a valley. But, after the heat and blast, there came the third killer, radiation, the most frightening of all because it kills silently and invisibly. At the moment of the explosion, alpha, beta and gamma rays, X-rays and neutrons were all given off. And, following the explosion, fission products such as strontium-90 and caesium-137 were scattered everywhere; these gave off further atomic radiation and held an ever-present threat to those who had survived the heat and blast. It is thought that, even if heat and blast had been entirely absent, the number of deaths within 1,000 yards of the Hiroshima and Nagasaki bombs would still have been almost the same. The main difference would have been in the time it would have taken for the victims to die. Those who were killed instantly might instead have survived a few days whilst the radiation destroyed their white blood cells and bone marrow.

Even today the people of Hiroshima and Nagasaki are suffering from the after-effects of the atomic explosions. On average, more dead and deformed children are born to the survivors than elsewhere. Survival after an atomic attack can be worse than death.

But death, that day, was much more common. Little eight-year-old Matsuo was happy that morning. He was playing hide-and-seek with six other boys, around the Chinzei Junior High School on a hillside in the centre of the Urakami Valley. Although he had been 'it', the one who looks for the others, for the last three games, he didn't mind. For this was the first time the slightly older boys had even allowed him to play with them.

Now Matsuo stood in the centre of the yard trying to spot the others hiding. When the bomb exploded some 400 yards behind him, he neither heard nor felt anything when the heat rays focused on him and obliterated him. The other boys, huddling in gullies, or crouching behind walls, were completely untouched by those same rays. Minutes later, they crept from their hiding places and walked to where the remains of little Matsuo's body lay on the ground. In horrified silence, they stared at each other. They were the lucky ones, or so they thought.

But once more the invisible killer was at work. Within one year, three of the six boys would be dead from radiation.*

Outside Japan, most people welcomed the news of the atomic bombs, as they seemed likely to end the war. Since then more and more people have come to agree with the words of Professor P. M. S. Blackett, the British physicist who won a Nobel Prize in 1948: 'the dropping of the atomic bombs was not so much the last military act of the Second World War, as the first act of the cold diplomatic war with Russia'. Thomas K. Finletter – who later became Chairman of the US 'Air Policy Committee' and head of the US Marshall Plan mission in London – explained clearly (15 June 1946) why there had been no demonstration of the new weapon's power to the Japanese government before it was decided to drop the bombs:

There was not enough time between 16 July when we knew at New Mexico that the bomb would work, and 8 August, the Russian deadline

*From *Nagasaki: The Forgotten Bomb* by F. W. Chinnock.

Einstein and Leo Szilard became prominent in campaigns for nuclear disarmament

date, for us to have set up the very complicated machinery of a test atomic bombing involving time-consuming problems of area preparations, etc. . . No, any test would have been impossible if the purpose was to knock Japan out before Russia came in – or at least before Russia could make anything other than a token of participation prior to a Japanese collapse.

Most of the leading scientists who worked on the first atomic bombs later regretted their participation. Szilard, Bohr, Einstein and Rotblat became prominent in campaigns against nuclear weapons. In 1955 eleven prominent scientists, including nine Nobel Prizewinners, signed a manifesto calling upon scientists throughout the world to work for peace:

> We are speaking on this occasion not as members of this or that nation, continent or creed, but as human beings, members of the species Man, whose continued existence is in doubt . . .
>
> We have to learn to think in a new way. We have to learn to ask ourselves not what steps can be taken to give military victory to whatever group we prefer, for there no longer are such steps; the question we have to ask ourselves is: what steps can be taken to prevent a military contest of which the issue must be disastrous to all parties? . . . Shall we put an end to the human race; or shall mankind renounce war?*

Bertrand Russell — Albert Einstein
Max Born — P. W. Bridgman
Linus Pauling — H. J. Muller
J. F. Joliot-Curie — C. F. Powell
Joseph Rotblat — L. Infeld
Hideki Yukawa

Following its publication the Manifesto was endorsed by hundreds of scientists and provided the impetus for an international conference to discuss the threat posed to the world by nuclear weapons. Out of the first conference of scientists, held at a small Canadian village called Pugwash, grew the Pugwash Movement. The conferences are now held regularly.

But, though the knowledge of the implications of nuclear

*From the Russell–Einstein Manifesto.

energy has become more widespread, not all nuclear scientists have shown the concern of those in the Pugwash Movement. Making nuclear weapons has become a living for thousands of scientists, technologists and production workers in this, the nuclear age.

By 1949 Russia had exploded her first A-bomb and in 1953 Britain joined the 'nuclear club'. The scientists involved do not appear to have been concerned with the moral implications. Nor were the politicians: on 1 June 1953 British Prime Minister Winston Churchill reported: 'We had one and let it off – it went off beautifully.'

2. Nuclear energy–how it works

They shall beat their swords into plow-shares, and their spears into pruning hooks: nation shall not lift up sword against nation, neither shall they learn war any more.

Isaiah 2:4

ballito STOCKINGS

News Chronicle

No. 30,958 TUESDAY, AUGUST 7, 1945 ONE PENNY

LATE LONDON EDITION

TUESday FIELD-DAY

On this Bank Holiday the course of world history may have been altered

FORCE OF NATURE HARNESSED: ATOM BOMB ON JAPAN

Power equal to 20,000 tons of T.N.T.

PUT ASIDE HIS TEACHING

SIR JAMES CHADWICK

ALLIES BEAT GERMANS IN BATTLE OF SCIENCE

From ROBERT WAITHMAN, News Chronicle Correspondent

WASHINGTON, Monday.

IT MAY BE THAT THIS BANK HOLIDAY WEEK-END THE COURSE OF WORLD HISTORY WAS CHANGED. FOR AT 11 A.M. IN THE WHITE HOUSE TODAY PRESIDENT TRUMAN ANNOUNCED THAT BRITISH AND AMERICAN SCIENTISTS, WORKING TOGETHER, HAD "HARNESSED THE BASIC POWER OF THE UNIVERSE," AND THAT A FEW HOURS EARLIER THE FIRST ATOMIC BOMB HAD FALLEN ON A JAPANESE CITY.

This is something so much bigger than any of the stories of war-time scientific discoveries that have yet appeared; its implications, for both good and bad, are still hidden.

President Truman says that "further examination" is necessary of "the possible methods of protecting us and the rest of the world from the danger of sudden destruction." More reassuringly, Secretary of War Stimson says that the means has been found of releasing the atomic energy "not explosively but in regulated amounts."

Equal to 2,000 of Britain's "Grand Slams"

But both Mr. Truman's and Mr. Stimson's statements make it clear that much more has still to be learned about the use of information that has been produced by the greatest scientific gamble in history.

Meanwhile its use in the form of the atomic bomb against the Japanese has been revealed with a great sense of drama. At about 7 p.m. yesterday an American plane flew over Hiroshima, a Japanese army base, and released the first bomb.

It was a bomb equal in power to 20,000 tons of T.N.T., or 2,000 times as powerful as Britain's "Grand Slam"—until now the world's biggest bomb, weighing 22,000lb.—and so powerful that it obliterated an entire island in the English Channel when it was first tried out.

Mr. Stimson said today that after the atomic bomb had exploded on Hiroshima reconnaissance planes were sent to the spot, but they found the target area covered with such "an impenetrable cloud of dust and smoke" that they had to fly back until the atmosphere cleared sufficiently for photographs to reveal what happened to the army base at Hiroshima, and perhaps to the nearby city and its 350,000 inhabitants.

Even more powerful forms are on the way

The Secretary of War went on to say that soon an improved bomb will be available that will increase "by several fold" the effectiveness of the present atomic bomb.

But "possession of this weapon by the United States, even in its present form, should prove a tremendous aid in shortening the war against Japan."

At the moment we are not being given any details of the bomb or its working. A warning has gone out from the Office of Censorship saying: "In the interests of the highest national security it is requested that editors and broadcasters continue to withhold information without appropriate authority concerning the scientific processes, formulas and mechanics of the operation of the atomic bomb; the location, procurement and consumption of uranium stocks; the quality and quantity of production of these bombs; their physics, characteristics and future military employment."

Work on the atomic bomb was carried out at two big plants and several lesser works in the United States, and at a 20,000-acre plant in Canada. A total of £500 millions has been spent on the work.

A little-known American Army expert, Maj.-Gen. Leslie R. Groves, directed the work under the innocuous title of "Commanding Officer of the Manhattan Engineer District."

Tens of thousands of men and women at the scattered plants had no idea what they were working on. It was the topmost of the top war secrets—and it was kept.

The Germans made efforts

Gen. Groves, in a statement here today said, "We knew there were definite and narrow chances throughout the entire programme. While we did not know where success would come, we knew it was worth doing, particularly after our Intelligence learned that the Germans were making efforts to solve the problem—how extensive we were unable to learn. It was the taking of calculated risks that paid."

Of the bomb itself, about all that can now be said—on the authority of President Truman and Secretary Stimson—is that uranium is the essential ore used in its production, and that the energy released is in the form of heat at a temperature effective for the destructive job that is now to be done, but ...

PROFESSOR NIELS BOHR

First atom bomb vaporised tower

WASHINGTON, Monday.

THE first experimental atomic bomb explosion in history took place on top of a steel tower in the desert of New Mexico, in thunder, lightning and rain, and scientists and military experts crouched in timber and earth shelters at the controls.

Zero hour was 5.30 a.m. on July 16 at the air base at Alamogordo, New Mexico.

What is meant by atomic energy

By a Scientific Correspondent

AN atom is the smallest particle of any element of matter, e.g., iron, oxygen, aluminium.

"IT CAN BE DONE," HE SAID IN 1941

SIR GEORGE THOMSON

TARGET, AND RESULT

British and U.S. scientists pooled skill

"THIS revelation of the secrets of nature, long mercifully withheld from man, should arouse the most solemn reflections in the minds and consciences of every human being capable of comprehension."

These serious words are contained in a statement on the new bomb which had been prepared by Mr. Churchill. The statement was issued by the Prime Minister, Mr. Attlee, from 10, Downing Street, last night.

"We must indeed," says Mr. Churchill, "pray that these awful agencies will be made to conduce to peace among the nations, and that, instead of wreaking measureless havoc upon the entire globe, they may become a perennial fountain of world prosperity."

Hidden cities housed the workers

Churchill's statement

Self-contained

Progress in 1941

Next step is to control the force

—Sir John Anderson

THE discovery of the atomic bomb is the greatest step forward ever made by man in his efforts to control nature.

Sir John Anderson, speaking as a physicist, told me this last night.

LATE NEWS

MACKENZIE KING SEAT SAFE

Only the key

LET the BELLS RING *but...*

Let the bells ring for the half is done! But after the bells a task remains.

While they still fight shall we forget— with a world to mend and wounds to heal?

The splash headlines of the *News Chronicle* for 7 August 1945 declared 'FORCE OF NATURE HARNESSED: ATOM BOMB ON JAPAN – Power equal to 20,000 tons of TNT'. A smaller heading on the same page said 'Next step is to control the force'. If we survive the twentieth century, the smaller article may prove the more significant. In it Sir John Anderson explained that the importance of the discovery of nuclear power

> far transcends that of the discovery of electricity and makes steam something of the far past. It has opened a new door to physics which has hitherto defied all approach. It means that man has at last found the way to release the forces of the atom.

Nowadays most people know in general terms that an atom is the smallest particle of any element of matter – for example, iron, tin, aluminium – and that all atoms are composed of neutrons and protons surrounded by electrons. The neutrons and protons (together called nucleons) form the nucleus of the atom and are kept together by nuclear binding forces. Protons have a positive electric charge and the number present in an atomic nucleus determines its chemical properties. So each chemical has a unique number of protons (for example, hydrogen has 1, helium 2, lithium 3, etc.) but the number of neutrons may vary. For example, although the ordinary hydrogen nucleus consists simply of 1 proton, there are two other forms (or *isotopes*) of hydrogen, called deuterium and tritium, which have an additional 1 and 2 neutrons respectively. It is the 'force of the atom' which keeps these neutrons and protons together in the nucleus.

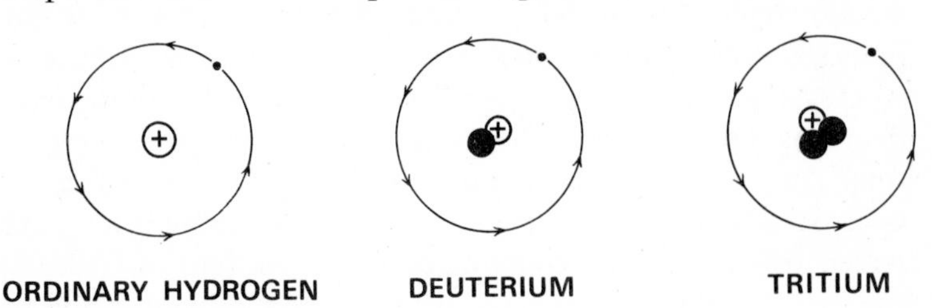

Atomic power

Nuclear energy is released when a heavy atom breaks into two (a process called *fission*) or when two light atoms join (*fusion*). Heavy atoms tend to be naturally unstable, because the nuclear binding forces find it difficult to keep the neutrons and protons together. Substances which are unstable in this way are *radioactive*. They emit radiations and are transformed into slightly different atoms. The rate of decay of a radioactive atom may be very low, sometimes it takes millions of years, but if such an

atom is given an extra jolt, for example by being hit with a neutron, it will break up instantaneously into two parts. It is this process of fission that can be used to make atomic bombs – like those dropped on Hiroshima and Nagasaki – or to produce electricity by nuclear power generation.

Uranium and plutonium were the chemicals used for the first atomic bombs. The nucleus of uranium contains 92 protons and, in its most common form (uranium-238), 146 neutrons. Uranium-238 ($92 + 146 = 238$) undergoes fission when hit by high-energy neutrons, but it can absorb low-energy neutrons without splitting. Another form of uranium, uranium-235, which has 143 neutrons, is much less stable. But natural uranium (i.e. that mined from the earth) contains only 0·7 per cent of U235. So the first step in the manufacture of an atomic bomb based on uranium, is to *enrich* the U235 component of natural uranium

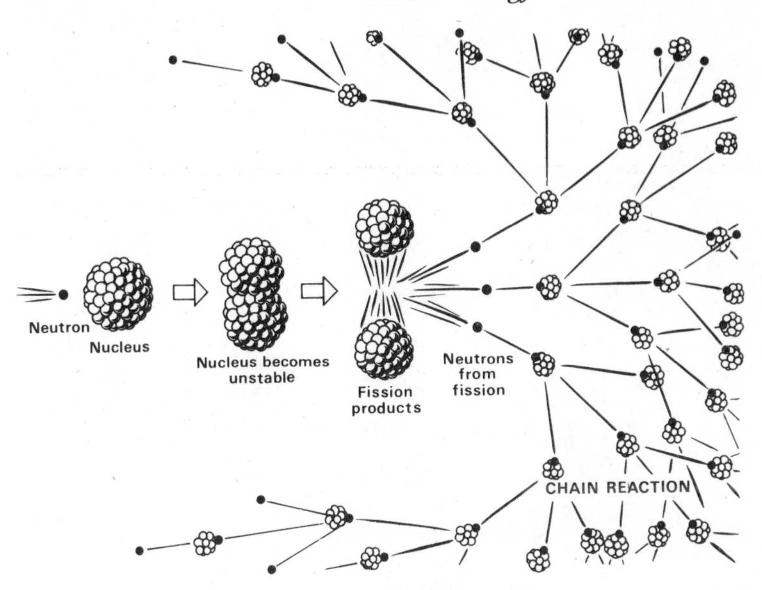

from 0·7 per cent to at least 70 per cent. When this is done, a self-sustaining *chain reaction* can occur in the uranium.

When the U235 atoms undergo fission they release energy as well as a few neutrons. These neutrons hit other atoms and in turn can cause these other atoms to undergo fission. On average 2·5 neutrons are given off from each uranium-235 atom and this opens up the possibility of a chain reaction. In effect, neutrons from one fission can induce fission in other atoms, in turn producing more neutrons. These neutrons produce still more fission and still more neutrons. So long as there are plenty of U235 atoms near by, this can go on and on. Within milli-seconds there is a tremendous release of heat.

This chain reaction continues only if there is sufficient uranium present. The amount needed for a self-sustaining reaction to take place is known as the *critical mass* (about fifteen kilogrammes in the case of U235). An A-bomb contains two or more lumps of radioactive material which are each smaller in size than the critical mass and are kept apart when the bomb is assembled.

Nuclear power stations and reprocessing plants in Great Britain

The atomic explosion takes place when these subcritical masses are brought together.

Fission is also used for nuclear power generation. In this case a slow, controlled, release of energy is needed and the composition of the uranium fuel is in most cases 1·5 to 5 per cent uranium-235, as opposed to the 70 per cent used in the atomic bomb. The amount of uranium is regulated so that the self-sustaining chain reaction does not 'take off'. This is, in effect, a controlled nuclear explosion, with the heat being removed to generate electricity in the same way as in coal-fired and oil-fired power stations. However, the *waste by-products* of nuclear power generation are more dangerous than those produced by burning oil or coal, because they are radioactive. Radioactivity is produced when some of the neutrons given out in the fission process miss uranium atoms, hit other substances and create new artificial radioactive substances. The main waste, however, arises from the two atoms into which the uranium atom is split. Both are radioactive. As the reactor goes on producing energy more and more of these radioactive fragments accumulate. For this reason the uranium fuel elements are removed after a time and the fuel material reconcentrated.

As more and more countries acquire nuclear power stations, the amount of radioactive waste material is growing. Many countries are unable or unwilling to make arrangements to reprocess this waste and it seems likely that only a few countries will build the necessary facilities. Britain has signed long-term contracts with Japan and other countries to handle the latter's nuclear waste products. Even after reprocessing, some radioactive waste remains and the only solution at present is to seal this in suitable containers for 'disposal'.

Plutonium

Plutonium on the other hand is a *useful* by-product of nuclear power generation and is made from the bombardment of the U238. It happens like this: when neutrons from the fission of uranium-235 hit atoms of U238, they are absorbed by the nucleus to produce another isotope – uranium-239 – which then undergoes its own radioactive decay process and eventually becomes plutonium (Pu239). For every gramme of uranium used in this type of nuclear power plant, about a gramme of plutonium is produced – and this plutonium is itself radioactive and can be used as fuel for further nuclear power generation. By choosing a suitable mixture of U235 and U238 and diluting the mixture with just the right amount of other non-absorbing atoms, the neutrons produced by the fission of U235 keep the reaction going to produce electricity *and*, simultaneously, plutonium from U238. By coincidence, naturally occurring uranium (99·3 per cent U238 and 0·7 per cent U235) *is* a suitable mixture and works just as described when it is diluted by pure graphite or heavy water.

So nuclear reactors can be built to produce electricity *and* to 'breed' new fission material. Future nuclear reactions may then use this plutonium to produce further nuclear energy. But, unfortunately, plutonium can also be used to make atomic bombs, and its critical mass is only 5 kg. Indeed the first atomic reactors were intended to produce plutonium; they generated electricity only as a by-product. The very first nuclear reactor started production in 1942 and within a very short time other nuclear reactors supplied the plutonium used for the Alamogordo and Nagasaki explosions. The Hiroshima bomb was the only one of the first three to use uranium.

In theory any radioactive material can be used to make an atomic bomb. In practice, however, plutonium and uranium are the most suitable starting materials for bomb manufacture. 'Peaceful' nuclear power plants thus enable countries to obtain plutonium for a nuclear weapons programme. India exploded her first atomic bomb with plutonium developed from the peaceful application of nuclear energy in cooperation with Canada, a country strongly against the spread of nuclear weapons. There is no way to stop countries from acquiring stockpiles of plutonium once they make electricity from nuclear power.

The basic arithmetic of the problem is as follows: a reactor that produces one megawatt of electric power can produce about a quarter kilogramme of plutonium per year. (Future nuclear reactors will produce *more* plutonium than they consume.) Nowadays it takes about 1 kilowatt of electric power to satisfy the needs of one inhabitant of a country like Britain. So, if everyone were to reach the level of the current British standard of living and if their electric power were produced by 'plutonium-breeding' nuclear reactors, the actual production rate of plutonium would be over a million kilogrammes per year. As it needs only about ten kilogrammes of plutonium to produce a fairly simple nuclear bomb, the annual production of plutonium in future could be equivalent to over a hundred thousand Hiroshima-sized bombs.

Although this number of bombs will not be produced, it will be extremely difficult to prevent plutonium losses and, indeed, a loss of the order of 0·1 per cent of the envisaged annual plutonium production probably would not be noticed. Even this amount in the wrong hands could make enough bombs to destroy many of the world's major population centres.

Wylfa power station on the north west coast of Anglesey came into operation in the early 1970s. It has a capacity of one million kilowatts and could supply enough electricity for the cities of Liverpool and Manchester

> The Atomic Energy Commission [of the United States] 'loses' about 100 pounds of uranium and 60 pounds of plutonium (the basic ingredients of nuclear fission) each year, which is sufficient to make about ten atom bombs.
>
> In most cases, when a loss is discovered, diligent clerical work usually corrects the error, but there have been instances where a loss has been attributed to espionage.
>
> Nearly fifteen years ago, an American nuclear plant 'lost' 207 pounds, enough to make several bombs.
>
> After a few months only 59 pounds had been recovered and, to this day, the AEC suspects that China or Israel may have acquired the remainder.
>
> Nuclear specialists generally agree that a government-owned nuclear plant presents a near-impregnable target for the nuclear terrorist.
>
> But as nuclear energy goes commercial, a number of privately owned energy plants will proliferate and will have only a fraction of the protective security of official plants.
>
> Nuclear scientists further conclude that materials in transit present the weakest link in nuclear security.
>
> This applies even to nationally owned plants in America, because once material has to be moved from one point to another, the national agent has to use private transport firms.
>
> In the year ending 31 March 1974, the AEC recorded 455 shipments of special nuclear materials carried by civilian contractors under licence.
>
> (from the *Western Daily Press*, July 1974)

Thermonuclear energy

To date, nuclear power plants have utilized nuclear fission as their source of energy. There are plans to develop *fusion* reactors to tap the energy released when two or more small atoms join together. However, commercial exploitation of this process is a long way off, since the temperatures involved are so high that

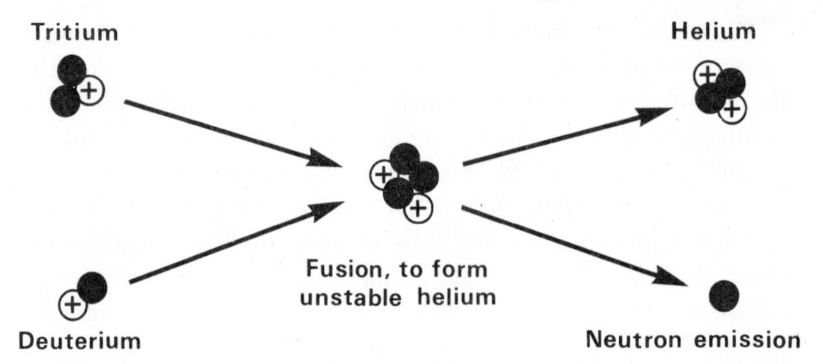

there is no known way at present to contain and control the reaction.

Unlike fission reactions, for which peaceful uses have been found, no one has succeeded so far in containing nuclear energy from fusion. All known materials melt and vaporize long before a million degrees centigrade is reached. Fusion actually takes place in the sun but is contained there by a blanket of thousands of miles of hot gas. With the technology available to us on earth the most promising idea is to keep the reaction within a 'magnetic bottle': in other words, to pass a very high temperature gas through a magnetic field and so tap the release of energy without any solid materials touching it. If this were successful, the world would have no need to fear an energy shortage in the future. Moreover this technique would not create undesirable waste products to the same extent as fission reactors.

But there *are* already fusion *bombs*. Thermonuclear bombs (H-bombs) are triggered by a vast amount of heat (the 'thermo' part) and work by the nuclear fusion of two or more small nuclei – for example, the joining together of two heavy hydrogen atoms to make helium. At temperatures of a million degrees centigrade or more, fusion reactions evolve vast amounts of energy. So a fusion bomb has big advantages over a fission bomb. Moreover, the size of a fission explosion is limited by the critical mass – if too much uranium or plutonium comes together the chain reaction will start too soon. There is no danger of this in a thermonuclear bomb; it can be as big and destructive as desired.

The way to obtain the heat to set off a fusion reaction is through a fission explosion. So an atomic bomb is needed to trigger a thermonuclear bomb! In effect a thermonuclear bomb is a fusion bomb encompassing a fission bomb. Whereas the power of atomic bombs is equivalent to thousands of tons of TNT (*kilotons*), the strength of a thermonuclear fission–fusion bomb may be measured in *megatons* (millions of tons of TNT equivalent). Most strategic nuclear weapons today are thermonuclear weapons in the range 0·1–10 megatons. (In addition, there are thousands of 'small', 'tactical' nuclear weapons, which are usually fission bombs in the 5–100 kilotons range.)

The development of the H-bomb

Most of the leading A-bomb scientists were not keen on the H-bomb – not even Robert Oppenheimer, who had directed the A-bomb project. When US President Harry Truman authorized its development (on 30 January 1950), Dr Edward Teller – the 'father of the H-bomb' – failed to entice more than a handful to come back to Los Alamos. Bethe and Fermi helped although they had strong reservations. But the brunt of the work was carried out by scientists who were less well known than the brilliant 'stars' of the wartime project and who showed little public concern with the moral implications.

The first experimental detonation was conducted in the spring of 1951 at Eniwetok, an atoll in the Marshall Islands in the Pacific (America had become too small for unconfined nuclear tests). There was some thermonuclear reaction, but most of the energy still came from fission. The second Eniwetok test, on 1 November 1952, was more successful and released energy equivalent to about 10 million tons (10 megatons) of TNT. It was reported to have blown an island off the face of the sea.

This test revealed, however, that the concept of a simple fission–fusion bomb was impracticable for military purposes. The thermonuclear fuels used in the experiment needed massive

The first experimental H-Bomb at Eniwetok Atoll, spring 1951

unwieldy refrigeration equipment and other complicated gear. Although the term 'H-bomb' is still used, the process of fusing hydrogen atoms (usually deuterium – 'heavy hydrogen') is merely a trigger for a secondary fission reaction.

The fission–fusion–fission bomb is an improved version of the thermonuclear bomb. First tested at Bikini Atoll on 1 March 1954, it comprises an ordinary fusion bomb, triggered by a fission bomb as described above, and encased in ordinary uranium. Although uranium-238 is unsuitable for a fission bomb, it can be induced to undergo fission by the very high temperatures of the fusion reaction. Because ordinary uranium is used, and there is no need to go through the expensive process of enriching it, the 'FFF bomb' has much more power for relatively little extra cost. From an analysis of the radioactivity released by the Bikini bomb, Professor Rotblat, by this time a vigorous opponent of the nuclear arms race, suggested that it comprised a plutonium core, a shell of lithium deuteride for the fusion reaction and an outer shell of U-238.

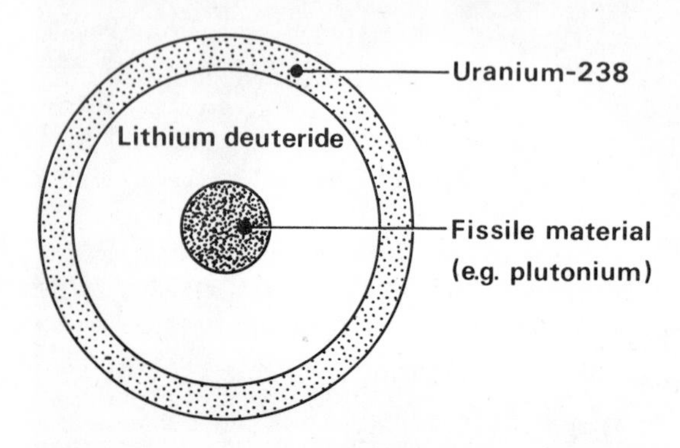

The voyage of the *Lucky Dragon*

Most of what is publicly known about thermonuclear bombs is due to an 'accident' to a Japanese fishing boat, the *Lucky Dragon*. Its crew of twenty-three were fishing for tuna some eighty-five miles east of Bikini Atoll when the first FFF bomb exploded.

> At 3.42 in the morning the lines had been thrown, and the Fishing Master again checked the ship's position. It was rather warm and the wind was east-north-east at two miles per hour . . . after ten minutes he signalled the engine room to stop the engine.
>
> In the darkness before dawn, the *Lucky Dragon* drifted on the calm Pacific, rocking gradually in almost imperceptible swells. It was a scene of serene peacefulness . . .
>
> On the bridge the Fishing Master peered through the sextant. The North Star was obscured, but he took a fix on other stars well known to him from past sightings . . . Glancing at his chart, Misake noted that the nearest point of land was the tiny island of Naen, forty miles almost due south. The boatswain was on the bridge and observed that the sky was starting to cloud over.
>
> Many of the crew, including the Captain, were asleep or were getting

ready for breakfast. Shinzo Suzuki, however, could not sleep; he awakened almost instinctively when the engine stopped and wondered if all the lines had been thrown. It seemed early for the night was still dark and it usually took much longer to complete the job. He called to a passing seaman and asked if the lines were all set. Upon learning that they were, Suzuki remembered the lost lines and realized that this accounted for the early completion of the job. It was warm and somewhat sticky. Suzuki, unable to sleep any longer, climbed out of his bunk and went on deck . . . He rested his arm on the roof of the after cabin and gazed absently into the somewhat overcast sky.

Suddenly the skies in the west lighted up and a great flare of whitish yellow light splashed against the clouds and illuminated the water. The startled seaman grasped the rough wood of the cabin with his hands and gazed in awe at the spectacle in the west. It seemed like minutes, though it was really only for seconds that he was transfixed by the dazzling light. It changed to a yellow red and then to a flaming orange red before Suzuki came to his senses and dashed back to his cabin to tell his mates what he had seen. As he entered the cabin, Takagi, a cabin mate, was humming a song. Suzuki blurted out, 'The sun rises in the west!' . . .

The men on the deck were not speechless, but jabbered in excited tones, 'It's a pikadon!' While another said, 'I wonder if it is a pikadon?' . . .

The fishing boat Lucky Dragon, *at her home port of Yaizu, Japan*

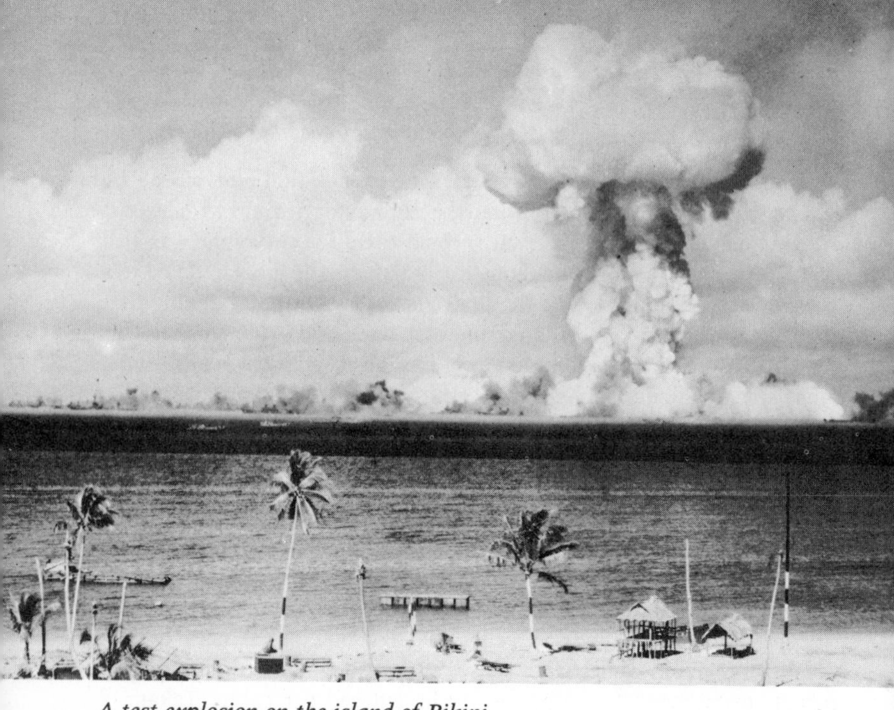

A test explosion on the island of Bikini

Everyone was shouting excitedly. 'What's the big red ball?' cried a shipmate. Another answered 'It must be the sun,' and was quickly doubted. 'No, it can't be the sun in the west!'

And again the word 'Pikadon!' was heard.

The glare in the west diminished in brightness as the colours seemed to spread out over the horizon and climb farther into the sky. No seaman had ever seen a sight like this before. Those who had crowded on deck after the first few minutes found it difficult to imagine what all the excitement was about, for by then the gaudy display of colours had faded or could be discerned with difficulty.

Captain Tsutsui was alerted by the burst of light flooding through the porthole near his bunk, but he was so drugged with sleep that he was slow to react. By the time he joined Misaki and the boatswain on the bridge the colour in the west had gone.

The darkness of the pre-dawn settled upon the shattered tranquillity of the tiny boat rocking in the limitless expanse of the Pacific. All was quiet. Gradually the crew's wonder turned to more mundane thoughts, namely breakfast . . .

They went into the galley, fetched some bowls of soup and returned to the deck, where four or five other companions were still discussing the event. Scarcely five minutes had elapsed. The men began to eat their breakfast. A few minutes later the ship seemed to tremble as though shaken from below and a great sound-wave enveloped the ship, seeming to come at once from above and below. This was followed in a few seconds by two concussions like distant rifle shots. Crewmen instinctively threw themselves on the deck and covered their heads . . .

The *Lucky Dragon* then proceeded on an east-north-east course to haul in the lines which had been set shortly before. Dawn broke before much of the line had been hauled up, and the crew relaxed somewhat as daylight helped to dispel some of their fears . . .

About two hours after they had started hauling the lines the sky began to change in a rather odd way. It was as though a high fog were forming. Then a light rain or drizzle started to fall. Except for two engineers at work below decks and the Radio man and Steersman, all the crew were on the main deck hard at work. They were puzzled at first when tiny bits of sandy ash came swirling down on the decks. 'It looks like the beginning of a snowstorm,' one of them said. The men kept working, paying little attention to the unusual rain. But it became bothersome, and the men blinked as the irritating grains of whitish sand got into their eyes. Some ash drifted down and touched their lips, deposited on their ear lobes, and dusted the men's hats.*

*From *The Voyage of the* Lucky Dragon by Ralph Lapp, Penguin, 1958.

Two of the fishermen from the Lucky Dragon

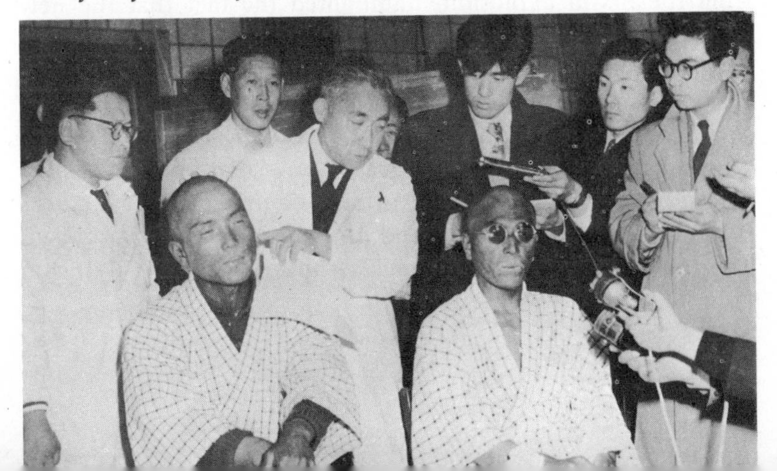

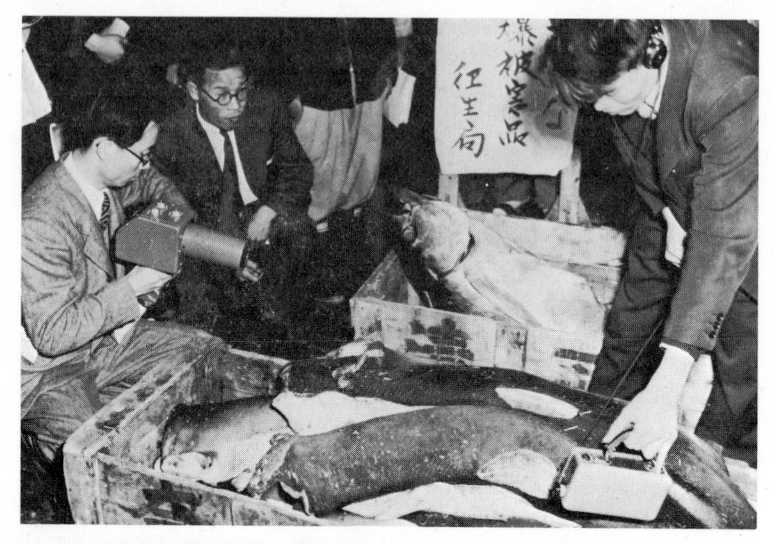

Fish being checked for radioactivity

When the ship reached port, some of the fish were sold before it was realized what had happened. Then radioactivity was discovered all over the ship and its cargo. Overnight the Japanese stopped eating fish. As for the fishermen, it was found that they had inhaled and swallowed radioactive fission products. All were sick and, despite intensive care, the Radio man Kuboyama died six months later.

The disaster that struck the *Lucky Dragon*, eighty-five miles from the Bikini explosion, highlighted the fact that the new bombs were very 'dirty' – that is, they emitted large quantities of radioactive material. The third and outer shell of the fission–fusion–fission bomb allowed the thermonuclear bomb to be made small enough for military applications but also threatened life after a nuclear war. It is estimated now that the radioactive fallout from only a fraction of present-day nuclear bomb stockpiles would be sufficient to end all human life on earth today. The new situation was quickly appreciated by Winston Churchill:

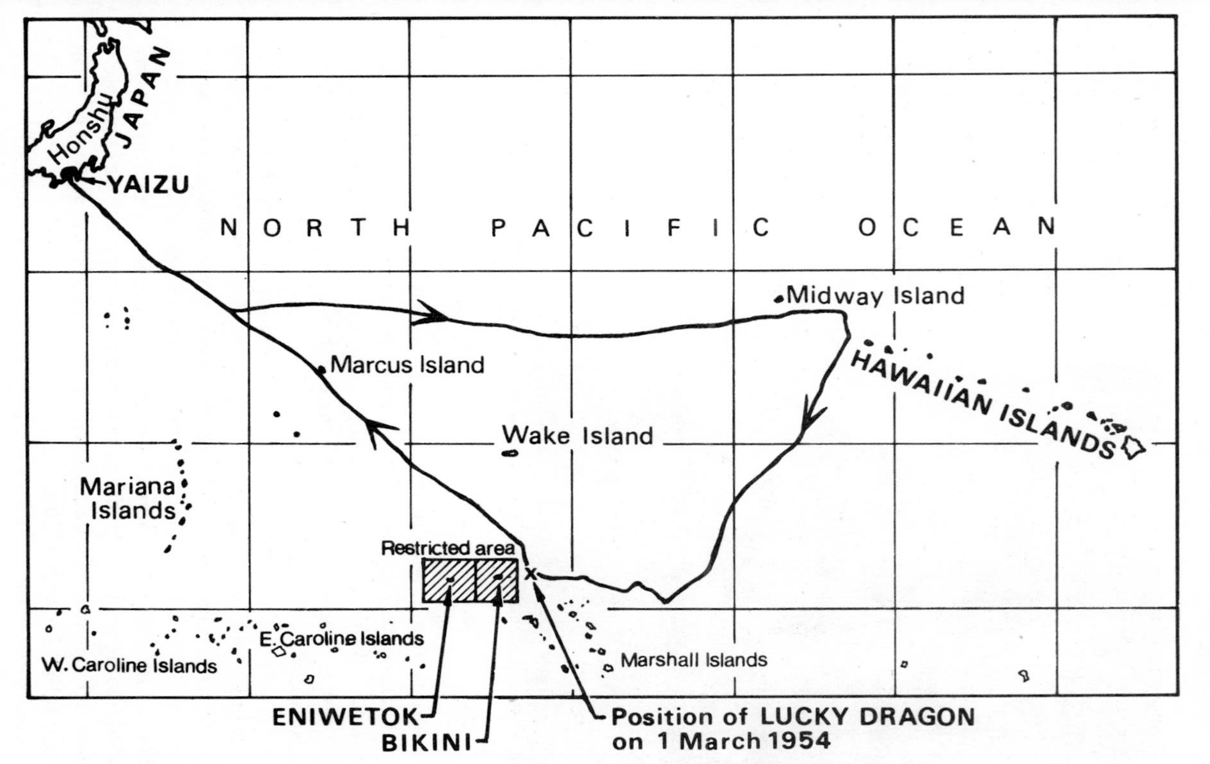

A map of the Lucky Dragon*'s voyage, showing its position at the time of the explosion*

Churchill in 1943

The atomic bomb, with all its terror, did not carry us outside the scope of human control or manageable events in thought or action in peace or war . . . With the hydrogen bomb, the entire foundation of human affairs was revolutionized, and mankind placed in a situation both measureless and laden with doom.

It is now the fact that a quantity of plutonium, probably less than would fill this box on the table – it is quite safe a thing to store – would suffice to produce weapons which would give indisputable world domination to any great Power which was the only one to have it. There is no absolute defence against the hydrogen bomb, nor is any method in sight by which the nation, or any country, can be completely guaranteed against the devastating injury which even a score of them might inflict on wide regions . . .

I find it poignant to look at youth in all its activity and ardour and, most of all, to watch little children playing their merry games, and

wonder what would lie before them if God wearied of mankind . . .
The problem is, therefore, to devise a balanced and phased system of disarmament which at no period enables any one of the participants to enjoy an advantage which might endanger the security of others . . .
The broad effect of the latest developments is to spread almost indefinitely and at least to a vast extent the area of mortal danger.*

Despite the risks of nuclear explosions, it is sometimes claimed that research should continue because it may have peaceful applications. The US 'Plowshare Program',† which attempted to find peacetime uses for nuclear explosions, showed this argument to be false. Conventional explosives proved more economical for long-trench digging, as for canals, and for relatively shallow excavations, as for harbours. Peaceful nuclear explosions were suggested also for oil-well drilling but, though this is technically feasible, the resulting oil flow is potentially radioactive. Similar objections exist for all other allegedly peaceful applications.

Yet although conventional explosives have been proved more practical, near-nuclear countries often pretend that they need nuclear-explosion technology for 'peaceful purposes'. In reality a country which develops nuclear-explosion technology is concerned above all with its destructive potential. In the twenty or more years since Churchill's warning, there have been *no* measures of disarmament which reduce the threat of the nuclear arms race. Shortly after America acquired her own H-bombs, Russia did the same and, in 1961, exploded the world's biggest thermonuclear device (57 megatons). Britain joined the H-bomb club by the end of the decade and France and China during the next (see the Table on pages 188–9).

Since 1961 tests of nuclear weapons have continued. With the development of lasers there is some prospect that a pure fusion

*Prime Minister Winston Churchill, House of Commons, March 1955.

†See the passage from Isaiah quoted at the head of this chapter. This is parodied in Joel 3:10: 'Beat your plowshares into swords, and your pruning hooks into spears: let the weak say, I am strong.' So far Joel has it.

bomb might be developed some time in the future. If this were to happen, there would be even less difficulty for additional countries to acquire nuclear weapons, since neither uranium nor plutonium would be needed. Perhaps these further developments are of no real consequence – world stockpiles of nuclear weapons already exceed 50 tons of TNT equivalent for every man, woman and child alive today.

3. Nuclear explosions

If we fight a war and win it with H-Bombs, what history will remember is not the ideals we were fighting for but the methods we used to accomplish them. These methods will be compared to the warfare of Genghis Khan who ruthlessly killed every last inhabitant of Persia.

Hans Bethe, H-bomb scientist

Nuclear explosions are not just very big bangs. There is a qualitative difference compared with conventional explosions. The reproductions on pages 50–51 from the British government's Civil Defence Handbook No. 10, *Advising the Householder on Protection against Nuclear Attack* (1963, now unobtainable), describe the basic facts of a thermonuclear explosion.

It does not quantify these various effects and appears to assume that there would be only one explosion. With a ten-megaton thermonuclear bomb the initial flash from the beginning of the fireball would be bright enough to blind temporarily and probably burn the eyes of people looking at it from 200 or 300 miles away. Within forty seconds a blindingly bright fireball would have grown about three miles across. This is where the thermonuclear reaction would be taking place and it would be as hot as the inside of the sun.

Then, depending on how high up it was when it exploded,

1 BASIC FACTS

What happens when an H-bomb explodes

The explosion of an H-bomb would cause total destruction for several miles around; the size of the area would depend on the size of the bomb and the height at which it was exploded. Outside this area survival would be possible but there would be three dangers:

HEAT BLAST FALL-OUT

HEAT An H-bomb explosion creates a huge white-hot fireball which lasts for about 20 seconds and gives off tremendous heat. The heat is so intense that it can kill people in the open up to several miles away. It could also burn exposed skin very much further away. Striking through unprotected windows it could set houses alight many miles away.

BLAST Blast would follow the heat waves like a hurricane. Buildings would be destroyed or severely damaged for several miles from the explosion, and there would be lighter damage for many miles beyond. There would be a further large area where, although houses suffered no structural damage, windows would be broken and there would be danger from flying glass.

FALL-OUT Fall-out is the dust that is sucked up from the ground by the explosion and made radioactive in the rising fireball. It rises high in the air and is carried down-wind, falling slowly to earth over an area which may be hundreds of miles long and tens of miles wide. Within this

5

From a Civil Defence Handbook

area everything in the open would be covered with a film of radioactive fall-out dust. Fall-out would start to reach the ground in the heavily damaged areas near the explosion in about half an hour. Further away it would take longer, and about one hundred miles away the fall-out might not come down for four to six hours.

Fall-out dust gives off radiation rather like X-rays. The radiation cannot be seen or felt, heard or smelled. It can be detected only by the special instruments with which the civil defence, the police and fire services would be equipped. Exposure to radiation, that is, being too close to fall-out dust for too long, can cause sickness or death. The radiation rapidly becomes less intense with time and after two days fall-out is about one hundred times less harmful than at first . . .

. . . but even then
it is still dangerous

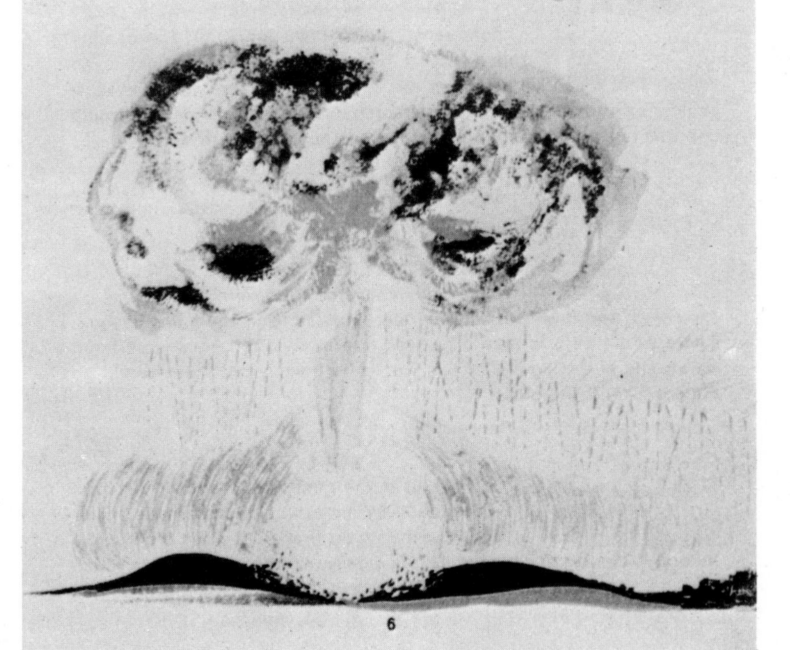

the bomb would create havoc for many miles around. If it was exploded very high up, where the air is thin, most of the bomb's energy would go into heat and it would thus be an effective fire weapon. A ten-megaton bomb exploded thirty miles up would send a searing wave of heat over an area of 5,000 square miles.

In a war most nuclear weapons are likely to explode near the ground – so the flash might not be seen further than thirty miles away. A ten-megaton bomb could produce a crater 240 feet deep (deeper than London's underground railway) and perhaps half to one mile across, with a huge rim of piled-up wreckage for up to twice that distance. The blast wave would travel along the tunnels of any underground system and so kill people sheltering in them ten or twenty miles away. People out in the open up to twenty-two miles away would be burned fatally; fires would be started up to twenty-eight miles away.

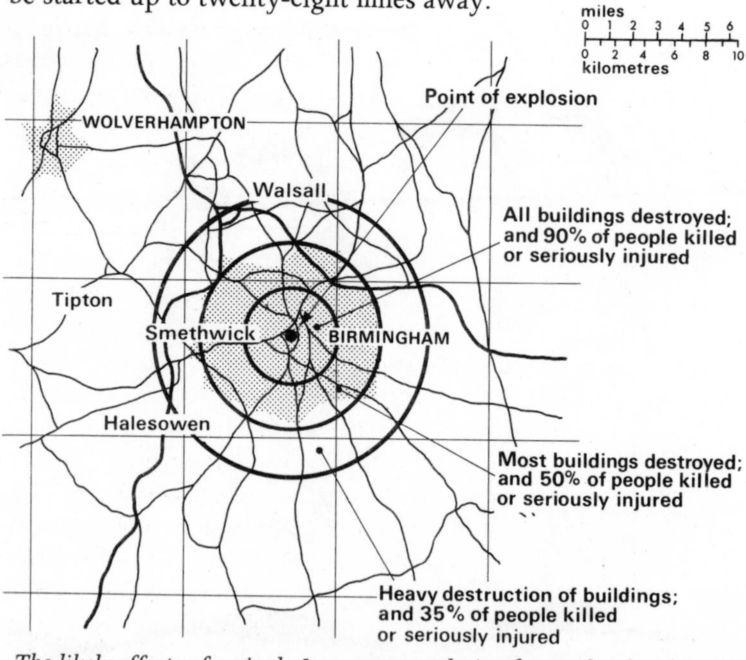

The likely effects of a single 1-megaton explosion from a height of 3,000 yards above the centre of Birmingham

Everything within three and a half miles would be totally smashed and there would be major damage to houses and streets up to fifteen miles away. People sheltering in basements or ground-floor rooms at this distance would be in danger from their homes collapsing. So the initial effects of blast and fire alone would be capable of killing over half the population of a city thus attacked.

Following this there would be further fire damage. The enormous number of fires that would be started over hundreds of square miles would not remain isolated. A 'firestorm' would be produced on a scale bigger than the big fire raids of the Second World War at Hamburg, Tokyo, Dresden and other cities, when the fires from thousands of incendiary bombs joined together to form huge pillars of fire which sucked in winds of up to 150 miles per hour (strong enough to uproot trees). People caught in the streets were burned to death and others in fire-proof shelters suffocated because the air that came in from the street was denuded of oxygen and scorchingly hot. Something similar, only worse, can be expected following a nuclear attack. The fire storm might well destroy everything within twenty miles.

People who survived the heat and blast would still have to face the third destroyer: radiation. There are three types from a nuclear explosion: alpha (α), beta (β) and gamma (γ) radiation. Alpha particles comprise 2 protons and 2 neutrons (in effect, the nucleus of the helium atom stripped of its electrons). A beta particle is a free electron given out during the decay of an unstable atomic nucleus. Gamma rays are high-energy electro-magnetic radiation, similar to X-rays, which are given out by many radioactive nuclei during decay. The intense burst of nuclear radiation from the explosion would create in turn numerous radioactive substances which would then give off further radiation. At Hiroshima, people who survived within a mile of the explosion centre died later from radiation sickness. In addition many others who were some distance away from the explosion centre died from radiation carried with the dust and debris many miles away.

IMMEDIATE DANGER from HEAT

TO AVOID BURNS

PEOPLE could be protected by being in shadow :

a. under cover or behind a solid object

b. covered by own clothing if no other shadow near enough to duck into

TO PREVENT FIRE

BUILDINGS could be protected at the first indication that danger was imminent, when householders would be asked to prevent fire by :

a. whitewashing windows to keep out heat

b. removing or flameproofing all materials that flame easily if exposed to great heat

c. having simple means of fighting fire, in the house

From a Civil Defence Handbook

DANGER from BLAST

Blast would follow quickly after heat. The siren warning would give time to take cover from both heat and blast. Choose the lowest possible place, preferably indoors, to avoid flying debris.

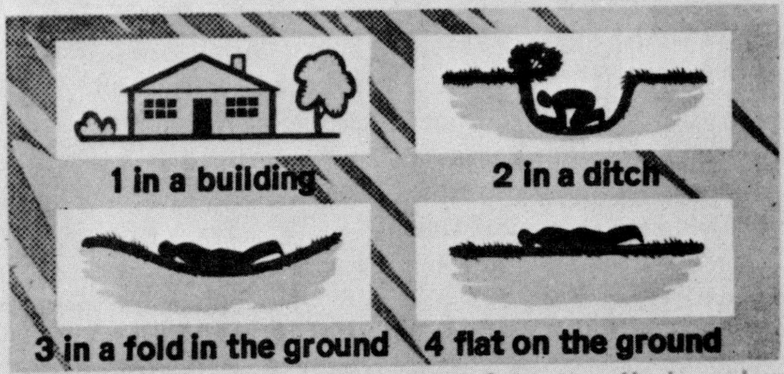

IN THE OPEN COUNTRY, less debris means that weaker cover could still give protection.

What happens is that the explosion sweeps up thousands of tons of earth and rubble and blows it up into the atmosphere forming the familiar mushroom cloud. The dust – fallout – settles back into the neighbourhood of the explosion during the next twelve hours. Radioactive nuclei are mixed with the dust so that a very wide area is dangerously radioactive – about 2,000 square miles for a ten-megaton bomb. This radioactive dust is extremely poisonous if inhaled and this is why you are advised to stay indoors for several days after a nuclear attack.

Radioactive substances giving off alpha and beta particles are only really dangerous when they get inside your body. Alpha particles can travel only a few inches in air and cannot penetrate skin. Beta particles travel no more than twenty or thirty feet in air and about one mm. through human skin. Both can be stopped by a thin sheet of material so, although these particles comprise much of the energy of a nuclear explosion, they are not a major additional hazard in its immediate aftermath.

Gamma radiation is the biggest radiation hazard just after a nuclear explosion. Like X-rays gamma rays penetrate matter and, although they get weaker in the process, they never completely disappear. People can be affected by gamma radiation some distance away from a nuclear explosion.

Large doses of radiation cause radiation sickness. The first effects are usually noticed within hours – sickness and vomiting. Later there is more vomiting, diarrhoea, weakness and mental depression. The hair falls out. Bleeding starts from the mouth, nose and bowels. Very intensive treatment is needed for recovery and this is not likely to be available under the conditions following a nuclear attack.

Nuclear fallout is also a long-term hazard. The fine dust from the mushroom cloud can stay aloft for two or more years and return to earth thousands of miles from the point of the explosion. Radioactive nuclei break up because they are unstable, but they do not break up all at once. It is a matter of chance when they do. Some exist in an unstable form for a long time (years), others for only a short time (days). (The really short-lived substances last

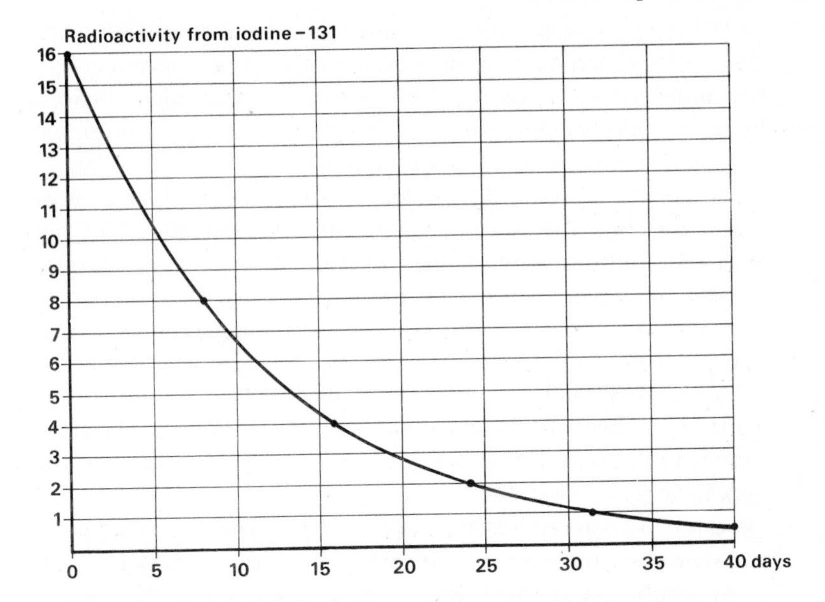

for only fractions of a second.) The nuclei obey the law of exponential decay – that is, in a given period of time a fixed fraction will decay. For example, for iodine-131, half will decay after eight days and then half of what is left after the next eight days, and so on. So iodine-131 is said to have a 'half-life' of eight days.

Some of the longer-lived radioactive substances in fallout dust can have even more serious effects than those previously described. The four most dangerous are strontium-90 (half-life: twenty-eight years), iodine-131 (eight days), caesium-137 (thirty years) and carbon-14 (5,670 years). These four are easily absorbed in our bodies, so that when they decay *all* their emitted radiation affects living matter. The effect is to change the chemical composition of living cells – a highly toxic form of internal poisoning.

The special danger of strontium-90 is that it is chemically similar to calcium and so is absorbed into our bones and blood. Growing children who drink milk from cows which have grazed on fallout-laden grass are especially vulnerable. So people born after 1955, when many atmospheric nuclear tests were conducted, have more strontium-90 in their bones than older people. By irradiation of bone marrow cells, or bone cells, strontium-90 may cause leukaemia or bone tumours.

Iodine-131 is like ordinary iodine and about 20 per cent of ingested iodine-131 accumulates in the thyroid gland. This can lead, especially in young babies, to stunted physical and mental growth. However, as it decays quite quickly (with a half-life of eight days), iodine-131 is not as great a long-term hazard as strontium-90.

Caesium-137 behaves in the body like potassium and is distributed through the soft tissue. It has relatively penetrating gamma radiation which can reach reproductive organs and thus present a genetic hazard.

Carbon-14 can replace ordinary carbon anywhere in the body and decays to nitrogen-14. So carbon-14, like caesium-137, can cause abnormal children to be born. Even today children of Hiroshima and Nagasaki are more likely to be born dead or deformed than elsewhere – the effects of radiation are transmitted to the unborn generations.

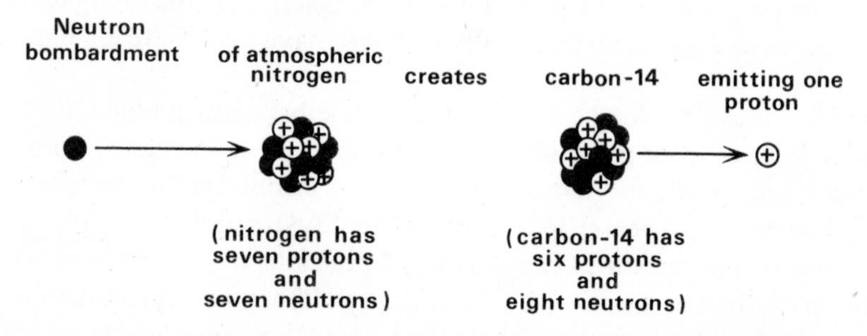

At one time it was suggested that a 'clean' bomb might be developed, so that there would be less danger from fallout. But 'clean' bombs – in practice, pure fusion bombs – produce particularly large amounts of carbon-14 as a result of neutron bombardment of atmospheric nitrogen (the 7 protons and 7

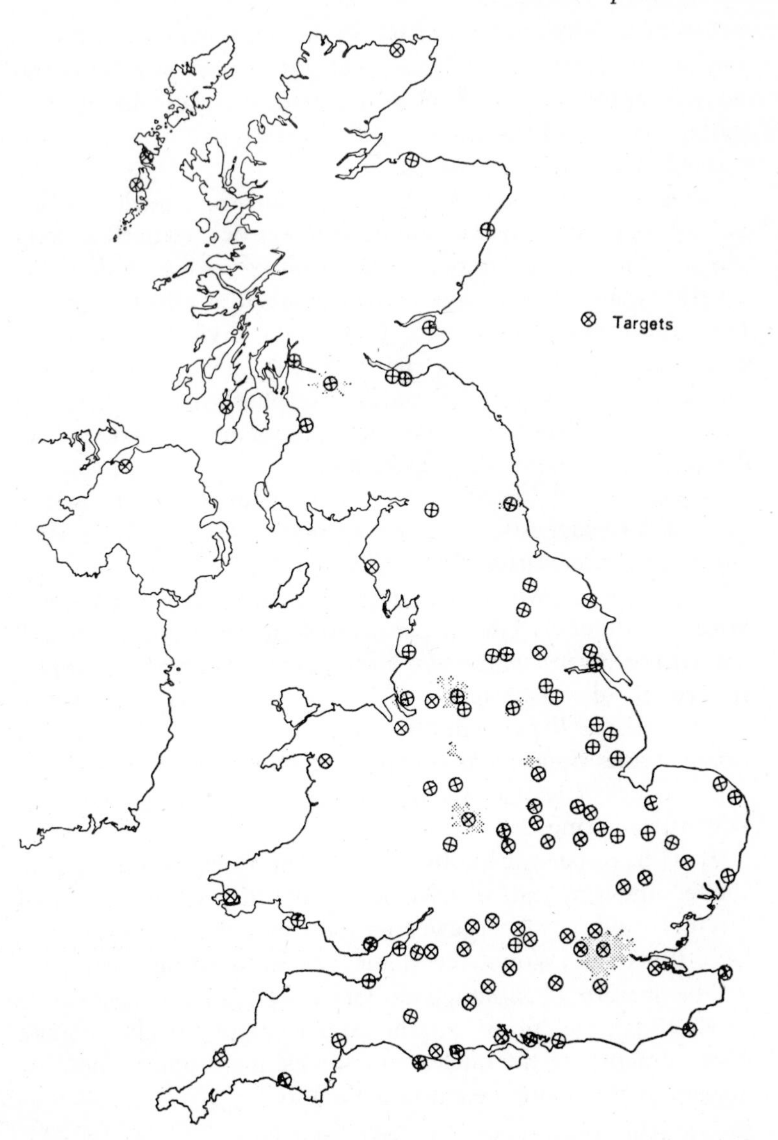

Possible British targets in a nuclear war. From Beneath the City Streets, *Peter Laurie*

neutrons of nitrogen become 6 protons and 8 neutrons which is carbon-14). Since carbon-14 has a half-life of 5,670 years, it would be present over *thousands* of years, with the result that genetic mutations would be spread over hundreds of generations instead of only one or two.

Altogether, the chances of survival following a nuclear attack are not good. Only a few H-bombs would be needed to effectively destroy Britain's main population centres and it is doubtful whether many people would survive the after-effects of radiation. The well-meaning instructions of the Civil Defence Handbooks reproduced in this chapter* only make sense for the minority that might be left on the periphery of one explosion centre. The instructions take no account of the wide-spread disruption of a full-scale nuclear war.

In a confidential memorandum to local authorities the British Home Office suggests: 'For the purposes of survival planning it could be assumed that the population survival rate would be 60 per cent in the worst areas and 95 per cent in the least affected areas.' Without civil defence measures they estimate the overall casualties at 80 per cent nationwide; with civil defence this might be brought down to 40 per cent; and with a national shelter policy perhaps 20 per cent. But these figures are *not* estimates of survival rates after a *major* nuclear war – they are estimates based upon a nuclear war so 'small' that survival planning would be worth attempting.

Plans have been made for an élite one in every hundred to shelter underground, if need be for months. But what sort of Britain would they emerge to after this time? Would any animals have survived? Would the water, gas and electricity supplies still be operating? Although military experts talk of 'acceptable levels of damage', for Britain the topic is hypothetical – no more than a fraction of the nuclear stockpiles in existence would be needed to annihilate the entire population.

*A new set of instructions was being prepared in 1976.

A prefabricated shelter costing 10,000 marks, capable of holding twelve people, on sale in West Germany in 1964. It is buried in a 15-feet-deep pit and is claimed by the manufacturers to be big and strong enough to allow its occupants to survive until danger is past

4. Non-nuclear weapons

International law limits the methods and weapons that belligerents may use against an enemy . . . all arms, projectiles or material calculated to cause unnecessary suffering and unnecessary death are forbidden. Poison and poisoned weapons are prohibited. Most opinion also agrees on forbidding dum-dum bullets (designed to expand or flatten easily in the human body), suffocating and poisonous gases, bacteriological warfare, and radiological weapons.

Regarding nuclear weapons, the preponderance of legal opinion has condemned the effects of nuclear radiation from these weapons as being 'akin to those inflicted by the use of poison or poisoned weapons . . . Thus, in principle, the use of such weapons is illegal' (International Law Association, Report of the Fiftieth Conference held at Brussels, 1962).

Most legal opinion does not regard the use of fire weapons such as flame throwers and napalm and incendiary bombs as illegal.

'The Laws of War', *Encyclopedia Britannica*, 1974 edition

Although nuclear weapons have not been used since 1945, their existence has profoundly influenced world events. The post-war period has been dominated by the nuclear arms race between the superpowers* with economic, social and military consequences for all other nations. Whilst they and their respective

*The USA and USSR are so far ahead of the rest of the world in military strength that it has become commonplace to bracket them together as 'superpowers'. The term 'leading nuclear powers' includes the superpowers and, usually, Britain – in recognition of Britain's advanced knowledge of nuclear explosion technology. The term 'nuclear powers' also includes France and China, and perhaps India.

allies have not risked direct confrontation, lesser powers have fought numerous 'small' non-nuclear wars. More people have been killed in these 'small' wars since 1945 than during any comparable period of 'peace'.

The danger of nuclear war may be one reason for this increase. The risk of universal nuclear war has to some extent restrained military action by the more powerful countries and this has helped smaller countries and guerilla movements to continue fighting against vastly superior forces. Although US generals advocated the use of nuclear weapons in Korea (1949–53) and Vietnam (1962–72), the politicians dared not provoke Soviet intervention in support of her allies.

In practice nuclear weapons are unusable for virtually all present-day conflicts. For example, in Northern Ireland they would destroy the very people who need protecting. If used on a battlefield, the troops of both sides would be destroyed. So for all wars except those between nuclear powers, nuclear weapons are inappropriate. (Apart from one other possibility: that terrorists might obtain plutonium and blackmail a major nation. Although this danger is real, it is nowhere near as serious as the main nuclear arms race.)

But nuclear weapons have influenced the *character* of modern warfare. In a nuclear war there would be no distinction between soldiers and civilians or between 'necessary suffering' and

"It was going to be the ultimate weapon, but I can't lift it."

'unnecessary suffering'. All the carefully worded legal definitions of humane warfare would be irrelevant, since friends, foes and neutrals would all die from radioactive fallout. By contrast, non-nuclear war can seem relatively humane (even when it violates previously accepted standards for conventional warfare). So under the shadow of nuclear warfare, conventional warfare has become far more terrible without evoking as much public attention.

Chemical and biological weapons

When a powerful nation fights a 'limited' war it cannot risk long-term effects like nuclear fallout. Moreover it is useful if buildings, factories and wealth are left untouched since there is no point in capturing a heap of useless rubble. Chemical and biological weapons (CBW) have been advocated as the best means of accomplishing this purpose.

Gas was used in the First World War, and the first extensive use of it then (in 1915) resulted in about 5,000 deaths. From then, until the end of the war in 1918, at least 125,000 tons of toxic chemicals were used, causing around 1,300,000 casualties of which about 100,000 were fatal. The gases used, mainly phosgene

The bodies of Russian victims of a First World War gas attack strewn around a German aid station

and mustard gas, were much less toxic than those available today and the means of delivery were very unsophisticated. 250 tons of VX (a modern nerve gas) could cause as many deaths as a 5 megaton thermonuclear bomb yet leave buildings, factories, roads, etc., undamaged.

Some lethal chemical weapons

Agents	*Mechanism*	*Speed of action*
Nerve agent G (e.g. Tabun, Sarin, Soman)	Interferes with nervous system	Seconds, by inhalation
Nerve agent V (e.g. VX)	Interferes with nervous system	Seconds, by inhalation, or minutes to hours through skin
Blister agent (e.g. sulphur mustard, nitrogen mustard)	Cell poison	Hours or days, but eyes affected more quickly
Choking (e.g. phosgene, cyanide)	Damages lungs	Immediate or up to three hours
Toxins (e.g. botulinus)	Neuromuscular paralysis	Hours or days depending on dosage

Biological weapons (BW) would be delivered in the same way as chemical gases, but the extent and nature of their effects are less easy to predict. Because they affect living organisms, bacteriological agents (germs) can be carried by migratory birds, animals and travellers to localities far removed from the areas originally attacked. Biological weapons therefore share the disadvantage of nuclear weapons: they could kill people on the attacker's side.

This disadvantage was also demonstrated by the phosgene and mustard gas used in the First World War – it was sometimes

CS gas is manufactured in crystalline form at Nancekuke, Cornwall

carried back by the wind. Nerve gases, which can kill by touch, suffer from the same drawback. So chemical and biological weapons are extremely risky and this is one reason why BW have been outlawed.

The BW Convention of 1972 prohibits all biological weapons

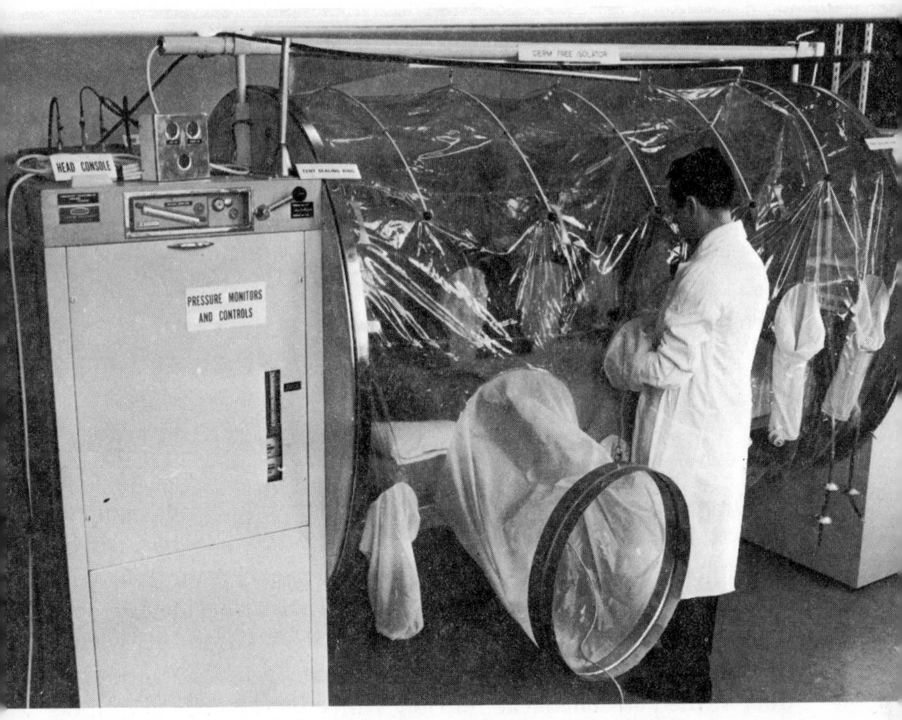

Equipment to maintain a germ-free atmosphere at Porton, Wiltshire

and provides for existing BW stockpiles to be destroyed. Unfortunately neither France nor China supports the treaty and we cannot be certain that even the signatory states have carried out its provisions. (Months after all BW were to have been destroyed, President Nixon learnt that US stockpiles were still intact – for 'technical reasons'.) Even if all the BW were to be destroyed, they could be easily prepared once again. The difficulty of preventing secret unofficial production – they can be made in a hospital laboratory – makes BW especially repugnant to the major powers.

Some lethal biological weapons

Agents	*Diseases*	*Incubation period (days)*
Viruses	Tick-borne encephalitis	5–15
	Yellow fever	3–6
Rickettsiae	Rocky Mountain spotted fever	3–10
	Epidemic typhus	6–15
Bacteria	Anthrax	1–5
	Cholera	1–5
	Pneumonic plague	2–5
	Typhoid	7–21

The production of poisonous chemicals is equally difficult to control but for a different reason. Many are widely used in peacetime – around 100,000 tons of phosgene are made in Britain every year for the manufacture of plastics, herbicides and pharmaceutical products. Ethylene oxide, 1 ton of which can be easily converted to 2 tons of mustard gas, is a major product of the petrochemical industry with a world-wide output of around 1,000,000 tons a year. Dimethylphosphite, which is needed to make the nerve gas Sarin, is used in the manufacture of pesticides. These examples show that it would be impracticable to prohibit the manufacture of chemicals that might be used for CW.

A more fruitful approach might be to prohibit the devices used to deliver BW and CW to their targets. A ban on rockets, bomber aircraft, bombs and shells would effectively prevent CBW being used. But it would also make atomic warfare impossible. So the effective prohibition of CBW is not likely until all ABC (atomic-biological-chemical) warfare is outlawed. Despite international law and the BW Convention, the threat of CBW remains.

Toxins appear to be the most effective and possibly the most efficient of the chemical weapons. A toxin is a chemical produced by a living organism. Its advantage is that it is non-contagious: that is, it cannot multiply like bacteria. It therefore has many of the advantages of a biological weapon without the disadvantage of uncontrolled growth. The Botulinus Toxin is 1,000 times more toxic than the nerve gases and before evaporating could wipe out all life in a given area inside six hours.

CBW are weapons of genocide: they cannot discriminate between armed forces and civilians. As few governments ever admit that they are fighting an entire population, this presents a big *political* disadvantage: the use of CBW is an admission that the vast majority of the population are treated as enemies.

So conventional bombing is still used. With conventional bombing it can be said that the prime targets are military – even when most victims are civilians. Similarly mines and boobytraps are often stated to have military targets. Although such statements are usually misleading – because soldiers are better protected than civilians from such weapons – this is one reason why 'conventional' weapons raise less political protest.

Anti-personnel weapons

However, for certain types of warfare, the intention can be to kill or deliberately maim *civilians*. The weapons used are known as anti-personnel weapons (APW) and have two major military advantages. In the first place, badly wounded people need food and medicine and need to be tended. Secondly, the dead and buried disappear from sight, whereas the injured remain visible as a constant reminder of the horror of the war. So APW sap morale and tie up valuable resources.

Incendiary weapons

Incendiary weapons (fire bombs), such as napalm, were the earliest anti-personnel weapons. They're not much good at destroying buildings and most military targets, but they are very effective against people. According to US military instructions the main object of fire bomb attacks is 'to kill, neutralize and demoralize'. (The manual does go on to mention that a secondary objective is to destroy 'or damage vehicles and equipment'.) Napalm, which is a jellified oily mixture, is the most well-known incendiary weapon and sticks to skin whilst continuing to burn. Magnesium and white phosphorus are newer types of fire bomb and have the additional property that they smoulder under the skin as the drops burn down to the bone.

Although napalm and similar devices have been used extensively for many years, there is some doubt concerning the legality of their use. A UK manual states 'their use against personnel is contrary to the law of war in so far as it is calculated to cause unnecessary suffering'. The US Army Manual, *The Law of Land Warfare*, states: 'The use of weapons which employ fire, flame throwers, or napalm, and other incendiary agents, against targets requiring their use is not violative of international law. They should not, however, be employed in such a way as to cause unnecessary suffering to individuals.'

In practice incendiary weapons are at least as useful as

On the Golan Heights. A destroyed Syrian armoured vehicle with a victim of a napalm attack

conventional explosives against people. So, despite the unnecessary suffering caused, napalm is normally employed against people. There may be some excuse for the production of napalm because it can be used against military targets. Other anti-personnel weapons do not have this justification. Fragmentation bombs, for example, cannot even puncture a truck tyre – although they cause people excruciating agony.

Fragmentation bombs

A fragmentation mine scatters hundreds of small pellets, or flechettes, which penetrate flesh and are not easily removed. Flechettes are irregular-shaped pellets which work their way through flesh like fishing hooks. So the surgeon who tries to remove a flechette cannot be sure whether it is still close to the point of entry. To make it even more difficult, some pellets are made in hard plastic which do not show up on X-rays and therefore cannot be found except by blind probing with a surgeon's knife. It is easy to see how such weapons use more medical resources than an equivalent attack with conventional explosives.

Gravel mines can be smaller than three inches square and are often covered with plastic or cloth. They explode when trodden on. These were used extensively in Vietnam. Whereas soldiers were protected by heavy boots, many a barefoot Vietnamese peasant lost a foot by these devices. The camouflage also meant that children were more commonly the victims – their inquisitive fingers sought out the scraps of cloth where adults walked past without interest.

Weapons which 'needlessly increase suffering' or which attack civilians rather than soldiers were outlawed as early as 1867 at the St Petersburg conference and this principle has been reaffirmed in every subsequent international agreement on the laws of warfare. Yet there was little outcry at their use in Vietnam.

Ecocide

The Vietnam War showed that even anti-personnel weapons and

conventional bombing could not subdue people determined to resist. They learnt to live underground in the jungle and under extremely primitive conditions. So further measures were attempted.

Bomb craters. Bein Hoa province, South Vietnam, 8 August 1971

Defoliation with herbicides (several years later). Gia Dinh province, South Vietnam, 10 August 1971

Vast areas of land were sprayed with herbicide under operations code-named 'Food denial' and 'Cover denial'. 'Food denial' was meant to prevent local farmers supplying food to the Vietnamese guerillas. 'Cover denial' meant stripping leaves, foliage and vegetation to remove the cover which gave protection from helicopter patrols. As a consequence vast tracts of land were destroyed for agriculture. Approximately one eighth of South Vietnam has been sprayed with herbicides and as a result much of this land will not supply food in the foreseeable future.

A vast expanse of woods [and] . . . crop-producing land [was sprayed] and more than 1,000 inhabitants were affected. A large number of livestock were also poisoned and some of them died. The majority of the poisoned people did not take any food from these crops nor drink any of the water that had been covered or mixed with the sprinkled germ chemicals. They had only breathed in the polluted air, or the poison had touched their skin. At first they felt sick and some had diarrhoea; then they began to find it hard to breathe and they had low blood pressure; some serious cases had trouble with their optic nerves and went blind. Pregnant women gave birth to still-born or premature children. Most of the affected cattle died from serious

Land levelling by Rome plough. Tay Ninh province, South Vietnam, 10 August 1971

diarrhoea, and river fish floated to the surface of the water, belly up, soon after the chemicals were spread.*

When defoliation failed to win the war, more systematic destruction was attempted. Land was levelled for perhaps a quarter of a mile on either side of highways and for half a mile round army camps and villages. Later, reploughing was encouraged to prevent the land recovering. As a consequence it has tended to harden by exposure to sunlight. In some areas the land solidified to rock and will never again be used for agriculture. This sort of attack upon the ecology of a country has become known as ecocide.

Conventional bombing also contributes to ecocide. Twenty-five million bomb craters have caused permanent damage to the landscape of South Vietnam, creating breeding ponds for disease-carrying mosquitoes. Few farmers risk walking between the craters for fear of unexploded bombs. The worst-affected areas are those that were subjected to 'carpet bombing'.

Carpet bombing was used by the Americans to maximize the damage on the ground and minimize the danger to their own pilots. Instead of attacking military targets one by one, formations of bombers flew together at a great height releasing their bombs at pre-set intervals. This laid a broad 'carpet' of bomb damage, equivalent in effect to ploughing a quarter-mile strip for miles and miles through the jungle. In addition to all the deleterious effects mentioned earlier with respect to bombing, ploughing and defoliation, the subdivision of the jungles prevents wild life and vegetation moving between the smaller areas left and makes recovery even more difficult.

The ultimate solution

With such weapons conventional warfare is not much different from a small nuclear war. Indeed the difference between

*From a South Vietnamese doctor's account of a chemical attack near Saigon, 3 October 1964.

ADSID (Air-Delivered Seismic Detection Sensor), the most widely used of the air-delivered sensors, detects ground vibrations caused by troops or vehicles. Information is then transmitted to a relay aircraft and thence to the Infiltration Surveillance Centre. This photograph, taken in Vietnam in June 1971, shows an ADSID (centre) *which is not easily distinguishable*

conventional war and nuclear war becomes blurred when 1,500-lb. conventional explosive bombs are used. The real significance is political. Once nuclear weapons are used, an all-out global war is almost certain to follow. So anything short of nuclear weapons has become 'conventional' and, by implication, acceptable – because it is not as horrible as nuclear war.

Yet the 'conventional' Vietnam war was more terrible than any preceding war. In terms of tonnage more conventional explosives were dropped on Vietnam than were dropped during the Second World War – quite apart from the chemical weapons used, the defoliation and the anti-personnel weapons. And, since the war was essentially a political conflict, there was no distinction made between soldiers and civilians or between 'necessary' and 'unnecessary' suffering.

Still the search goes on to find a technique, short of nuclear war, that would enable a powerful country to subdue a determined people. New ways are being developed to protect a sophisticated military force from retaliation.

The electronic battlefield is the ultimate solution. Instead of risking troops and manned helicopters and planes, pilotless aircraft will drop electronic gadgets all over the country from a great height. The gadgets will be equipped with listening and sensing devices, and perhaps roving television cameras which transmit signals back to command bases. Pilotless bombers will then be dispatched to attack targets selected by computers supplied with this field data. In this way no lives need be lost by the attacking power.

> On the battlefield of the future, enemy forces will be located, trapped and targeted almost instantaneously through the use of data links, computer-assisted intelligence evaluation and automated fire control . . . I am confident the American people will welcome and applaud the developments that will replace, wherever possible, the man with the machine.*

*General William Westmorland, to an American Congressional committee, 1970.

General William C. Westmorland, Commander of US forces, in South Vietnam in 1965

Some of these gadgets have already been tested and used. But they were somewhat primitive and the resourceful Vietnamese devised counter-measures. They moved the gadgets around, left motors running close to acoustic sensors and hung bags of urine from trees to overload the sensors which detected smells. Although a lot was learnt, the techniques were not much use at that time.

Nor would these devices have been effective against a technologically advanced adversary. The methods depend upon a gross disparity in the relative strengths of the two forces. Neither America nor Russia would attempt to drop sensors over each other's territories for fear of provoking a nuclear war. So the genocide and ecocide of 'conventional' non-nuclear war is only feasible nowadays against guerilla movements and relatively weak military forces. The nuclear arms race remains top priority for the two leading military powers.

5. Missiles and military strategy

With no advantage to be gained by striking first and no disadvantage to be suffered by striking second, there will be no motive for surprise or pre-emptive attack. Mutual invulnerability means mutual deterrence. It is the most stable position from the point of view of preventing all-out war.

Henry Kissinger

From about 1955 onwards the arms race has been concerned primarily with missiles and delivery systems. Although bombs can be made more powerful than 57 megatons, a scatter of smaller bombs can cause just as much destruction. With tens of tons of TNT explosive equivalent for every man, woman and child alive in the world today, the USA and USSR do not need more nuclear explosives. For them it is far more important to ensure that bombs land on target. Developments in technology, to make bombs smaller, enable delivery vehicles to become more effective in range and accuracy.

Alongside such developments in technology there have been changes in military strategy. Victory in a nuclear war must mean *total* destruction of the enemy – otherwise the other side can retaliate and the 'victor' may be as badly affected as the vanquished. So it is better to be the attacker in a nuclear war: the only way to 'win' is to launch a surprise attack so powerful that the enemy cannot retaliate.

In the jargon of nuclear strategy, plans for a surprise attack are known as *first-strike strategy* and the ability to launch a successful first strike is known as *first-strike capability.* The response is to protect nuclear weapons so that there are always enough left (even after a nuclear attack) to hit back and inflict widespread destruction throughout the attacker's country. Provided this *second-strike capability* exists, and is known to exist, a sane military strategist will be deterred from starting a nuclear war. *Mutually assured destruction* (MAD) means that the world is safe!

Jargon

It is unfortunately necessary to learn terms like 'first strike', 'second strike' and 'mutually assured destruction' to follow the arguments of military strategists. (Examples of these terms appear overleaf.) However, they can be very misleading if accepted at face value. For example:

*A 'tactical nuclear weapon' can be bigger than the atomic bomb that destroyed Hiroshima.

*A 'limited nuclear war' could have more casualties than the First and Second World Wars combined.

*An 'acceptable level of damage' can mean more than 40 per cent of a population killed (e.g. 20 million dead in Britain).

*A 'counter-force' strategy involves attacks on military targets and is essentially a strategy to start a nuclear war.

*A 'counter-city' strategy involves attacks on civilians and is essentially a strategy to deter a nuclear war.

These last two examples are worth examining more fully as they illustrate how jargon makes policies seem more reasonable than they are. Mass murder ('counter-city') seems worse than destruction of weapons ('counter-force'). However, military targets are appropriate only if the intention is to launch a first strike. These targets have to be destroyed before the enemy becomes aware that he is being attacked and retaliates. If, on the other hand, the point is to deter the opponent from attacking, it is ridiculous to aim at military targets – they will be empty at the time of retaliation, since the opponent will have used his weapons for his first strike.

So a counter-force strategy actually means a strategy for starting a nuclear war, whereas a counter-city strategy is one based on retaliation. The USSR has always lagged behind the USA in the nuclear arms race and boasts of the size of its nuclear warheads and of how many people it can kill (counter-city). By contrast the USA boasts of its missile accuracy and of how many military bases it can destroy (counter-force). Although it is certainly reprehensible to threaten mass annihilation (even in retaliation), a threat to start a nuclear war and initiate mass destruction is no better. In July 1975 US Defense Secretary James Schlesinger confirmed this point explicitly: 'Under no circumstances could we disavow the first use of nuclear weapons.'

Offensive and defensive weapons

The term 'defensive weapon' is another misleading piece of military jargon – it sounds rather soothing and almost nice. In reality, 'defensive weapons' are – if that is possible – even more of a threat than 'offensive weapons'.

'Offensive weapons' are intended for attack against military bases, towns, etc., while 'defensive weapons' are intended to repel such an attack (for example, by destroying attacking missiles). But the reason for developing 'defensive' weapons could be to ward off retaliation – to make a first strike feasible. (Conversely a second-strike strategy requires 'offensive' weapons to penetrate defences and so deter aggression.)

So 'defensive weapons' are not 'good'. An effective defensive system would enable an attack to be launched. Every weapon has a purpose *in the context of military strategy*: there are no peaceful nuclear weapons as such.

Nuclear language

Excerpts from the Press Conference of US Secretary of Defense James Schlesinger, 10 January 1974

Q. Could you amplify on the changing in targeting strategy?

A. I think that this has been discussed over the years, that to a large extent the American doctrinal position has been wrapped around something called 'assured destruction', which implies a tendency to target Soviet cities initially and massively and that this is the only option that the President of the United States or the national command authorities would have in the event of a possible recourse to strategic weapons. It is our intention that this not be the only option and possibly not the principal option open to the national command authorities.

Q. Can you just go a little further and tell me what you're talking about? What are you trying to do that is different? What is the change? What is the other option?

A. I'm not going to spell that out to you right now.

Q. Well, could you put it in English then, so that a layman can understand what you're driving at?

A. The main point that should be understood is that both sides now have, and will continue to have, invulnerable second-strike forces, and that with those invulnerable second-strike forces it is inevitable, or virtually inevitable, that the employment by one side of its forces against the cities of the other side in an all-out strike will immediately bring a counter-strike against its own cities. Consequently, the range of circumstances in which an all-out strike against an opponent's cities can be contemplated has narrowed considerably and one wishes to have alternatives for employment of strategic forces other than what would be, for the party initiating, a suicidal strike against the cities of the other side.

Q. You didn't mention it specifically, but I think it's a fact that for a long time both sides have had vast capability of overkill. You have mentioned and emphasized today that both sides are invulnerable as to second-strike capabilities. Given those two facts why is it necessary for us to match the Soviets on every front of extension – which to me . . . looks like spiralling increase in armaments, rather than balance?

A. Overkill is an expression which is part and parcel of the belief that the only objective – the only target – for nuclear forces should be the populations, the industry and the cities on the other side. That refers back to a point of view about the hypothetical employment of strategic forces which has known various names over the years – assured destruction, massive retaliation and the like. If one is thinking only in terms of the ability to bash the cities on the other side, we have more than enough forces . . . One does not necessarily have to go after a large set of targets, one must be in a position that one can respond in the event – in the hypothetical event of hypothetical aggression – with the strategic forces preferably in a way that limits damage to both sides – to all sides – rather than in a way that hopefully reduces the possibility of that outcome by flamboyant advertising of the destructiveness of such a war.

Q. Are you not talking about the possibility of tactical nuclear weapons again?

A. The answer to that is the observations that I've made about the need for selectivity and constraint, designed to . . . minimize collateral damage and to avoid to as great an extent as possible bystander fatalities, applies as well to tactical nuclear warfare as to strategic warfare. It applies fully as well.

Missiles

The first atomic bombs were dropped from aircraft. But bombers have become increasingly vulnerable to anti-aircraft defences and they are, by modern standards, slow. (The fastest bombers would take several hours on the journey between Moscow and New York whereas missiles could arrive within the hour.) Since the late 1950s more and more reliance has been placed upon missiles – indeed the impetus for the space race began with military rockets rather than a desire for scientific exploration.

Titan II missile on launch pad

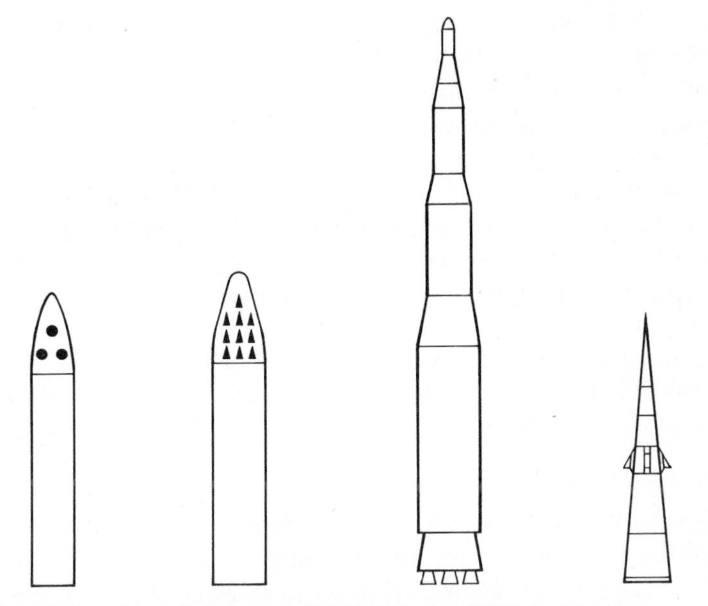

The relative sizes of: (left to right) *Polaris (an SLBM with three 200-kiloton warheads); Poseidon (SLBM with ten 50-kiloton warheads); Minuteman 2 (ICBM with three 200-kiloton warheads) and Sprint (an ABM)*

The first missiles were not very accurate over the USSR/USA range and so could not be used against small targets – only against large cities. But nowadays missile accuracies are to within 200 yards (by 1980 perhaps thirty yards) and it is possible for an Intercontinental Ballistic Missile (ICBM) to destroy a hard military target.

Missiles are now kept at instant readiness for firing. Formerly firing took several hours, thus giving the aggressor a big advantage: in theory the attacker could have destroyed all enemy missiles whilst they were still on their launch pads. (In response to this, missiles are now programmed to fire simultaneously and to leave their silos before the attacking missiles arrive.)

As well as ICBMs there are intermediate-range ballistic missiles (IRBMs) which, for example, could hit Moscow from missile sites in Europe or Turkey; and submarine-launched ballistic missiles (SLBMs) which, in 1975, had ranges of 1,500 to 3,000 miles. Many of these missiles are able to deliver several nuclear warheads at once, spraying their targets as if with nuclear grapeshot.

All the missiles so far mentioned follow ballistic trajectories: that is, after the initial thrust, they proceed to their targets under free-fall conditions. By 1980 many intercontinental missiles may be powered throughout their flight ('cruise missiles') with automatic navigation equipment on board to make course corrections as required. The cruise missiles are potentially far more accurate than the ballistic missiles and, if successfully deployed, would make ICBMs obsolete.

Anti-ballistic missiles

Anti-ballistic missile (ABM) systems are intended for 'defence' against free-fall missiles carrying nuclear warheads. It is not practicable to score direct hits on missiles coming at a speed of more than 2,000 miles per hour. But if *nuclear* warheads are used in 'defence', even a 'near miss' of, say, five miles can destroy an enemy missile. The burst of neutrons and gamma radiation from the 'defensive explosion' makes up for any inaccuracy.

Every military move has its counter-move. One reply to ABM has been to load several nuclear warheads on a single missile. When the ICBM nears its target, it separates into several

An ABM system

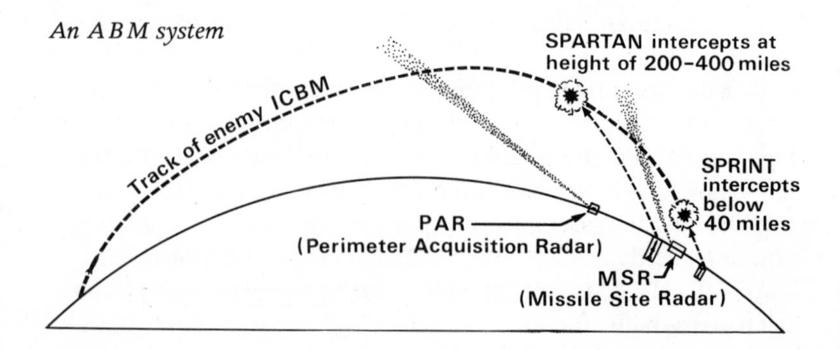

fragments, each with a nuclear warhead. By then it may be too late to launch the extra anti-missile missiles and extremely difficult to decide where each should be aimed.

Missiles with many nuclear warheads are known as MRV missiles (Multiple Re-entry Vehicles). In their crudest form these allow the attacker to spread the destruction more economically over a wider area. Whereas the 1962 version of a Polaris missile carried a single 800-kiloton warhead with each of its missiles, the 1964 version was able to deliver three 200-kiloton MRV warheads. Although the total explosive power was less (600 kilotons), its capacity to cause death and destruction was considerably greater.

MIRV

But MRV warheads are not very accurate. The next development has been MIRV (Multiple Independently targeted Re-entry Vehicles). In this instance each re-entry vehicle has its own guidance system aimed at a predetermined target. It is now possible to pack ten or more MIRVed nuclear warheads on a single missile.

Other techniques have been suggested to avoid ABM defences. A forerunner missile might explode a nuclear warhead to black

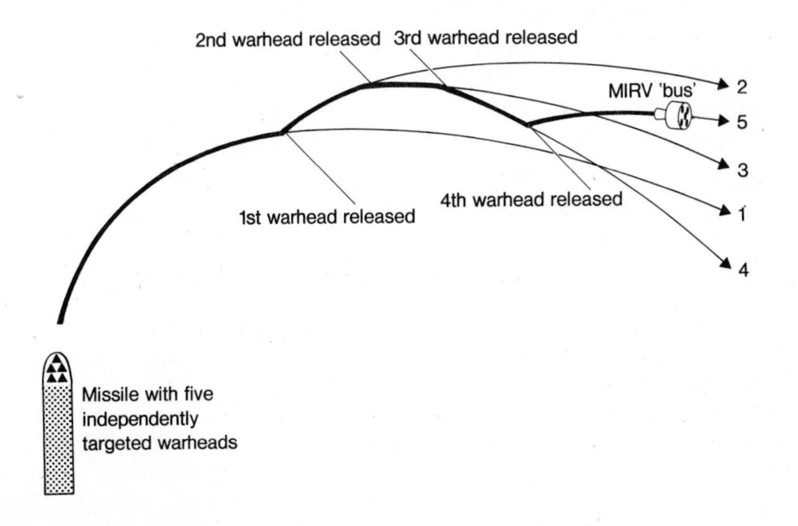

out ABM radars (an anti-anti-missile missile!). 'Decoy' objects might be used to overload the ABM system computers with spurious data. A further potential development of the MIRVed ICBMs is MARV (Manoeuvrable Re-entry Vehicles) which will change course to avoid the defensive ABM nuclear missiles. Both MIRV and MARV marry the proven worth of ballistic missiles with the newer developments in cruise-missile technology.

As a consequence of all these developments it is now thought that ABM defences are probably impracticable and, in 1972, the Soviet Union and United States agreed not to waste too much more money on this aspect of the nuclear arms race. But, although MIRVs were said to have been developed to counter ABMs, this agreement to control ABMs did not mean that MIRVs were abandoned – quite the contrary. And the strategic consequences of MIRV are, in some ways, the most serious aspect of the ongoing arms race.

This can be illustrated by considering the nuclear balance that would exist if both sides had 1,000 ICBMs, with one ICBM at each missile site, and these were the only nuclear weapons in existence. Neither could then risk a first-strike attack as this would need 100 per cent accuracy. At present there is no more than a 90 per cent probability that an ICBM will destroy a protected military target. So an attack of 1,000 ICBMs against the same number of missile sites would leave about 100 untouched, and these could then be used in retaliation by the defender. Thus equality in ICBM numbers would allow *both* sides to have a second-strike capability, which is, as Henry Kissinger says, 'the most stable position from the point of view of preventing all-out war'.

The way to improve 'kill probability'* is to make more

*'Kill probability' is the k-value calculated on pages 100–101. A 5-kiloton bomb with an accuracy of 50 yards has a 96 per cent probability of destroying a missile silo hardened to withstand an overpressure of 300 pounds per square inch. In 1975 about half the US silos and all the Soviet silos were vulnerable to nuclear warheads of such strength and accuracy.

accurate missiles or to increase the explosive strength of the nuclear warheads. This can be countered by better protection for missile sites so that they can withstand bigger explosive pressures. So far it has proved simpler and cheaper for the potential defender to improve his missile protection than for the attacker to achieve greater accuracy.

Another way to increase overall kill probability is to fire more missiles. With 2,000 missiles the probability of destroying the 1,000 missile silos would be raised to 99 per cent; with 3,000 missiles it would be 99·9 per cent. This illustrates that, for success, a first strike needs far more attacking warheads than there are targets. For the simple case of ICBMs only this would be extremely difficult to achieve – fortunately for world peace.

But with MIRVed warheads the chances of a successful first strike become more favourable, since 1,000 missiles could deliver ten times as many MIRVed nuclear warheads. Thus *both* sides could achieve a first-strike capability and *neither* side would have an effective second strike.

So the development of MIRV, though only part of the nuclear arms race, is a serious threat to the nuclear stalemate.

Missile protection

ICBMs are built underground in deep silos for protection. Most of America's 1,064 ICBMs are stored in hardened silos so well protected that a 1-megaton nuclear bomb would need to fall within about a quarter of a mile to damage the missile. Yet, with the improvements in missile accuracy claimed for the 1980s, it is believed that even this degree of protection will prove inadequate.

'Mobile launchers' are not as accurate as ICBMs but they are increasingly favoured as *second-strike* weapons because of their relative invulnerability to attack. They include ships, aircraft and submarines. Of these, ships have seemed the least important because they are slow moving and easily spotted. Their advantage is size: a single ship could carry hundreds of cruise missiles. Since warships can be easily destroyed,

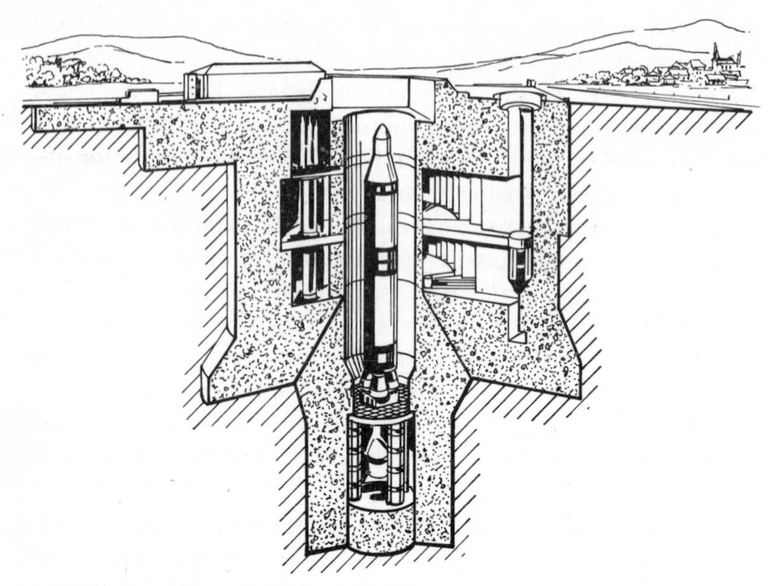

An underground missile silo

they are significant only in relation to a first-strike strategy.

Aircraft

Perhaps unexpectedly, bomber aircraft still have a future. This is due partly to the development of faster long-range aircraft but, more important still, to the introduction of short-range attack missiles (SRAMs) which replace conventional bombs. Using SRAMs, the aircraft need not get much closer than 100 miles to their targets and so they are almost invulnerable to anti-aircraft defences. The SRAMs are cruise missiles with their own guidance mechanisms – just like MIRVed warheads of ICBMs.

B-52 and FB-111 strategic bombers can carry twenty and six SRAMs respectively and thus, potentially, they more than double the number of nuclear warheads that America can deliver on Russia. At the time of writing, Russia has no comparable weapons. She would also need bases closer to America, in Canada and Mexico for example, to be able to threaten America with such short-range missiles.

It is likely that Russia will develop SRAMs but, by the time she has found some way to deploy the aircraft, America will have the new supersonic B-1 intercontinental strategic bomber, armed with thirty SRAM missiles and replacing the B-52s and FB-111s. Moreover America has already test-fired an ICBM from a C-37 Galaxy aircraft and thus seems likely to remain ahead in the field of air-launched missiles for the foreseeable future.

Not to be completely outdone, Britain, Italy and West Germany were, in 1976, cooperating to produce hundreds of Multi-Role Combat Aircraft (MRCA) which could be used to carry thermo-nuclear bombs. At the prices then prevailing the 400 MRCA for Britain would cost £4,000 million.

Submarines

Nuclear submarines are highly effective second-strike weapons. They are nuclear in two senses: they fire nuclear warheads and they are powered by nuclear reactors. They can stay underwater for three months at a time and, except when in shallow water or close to islands, are undetectable by current technology. Their role is to continue on patrol underwater for long periods – even after a nuclear war in which their home country may have been destroyed. This invulnerability makes them ideal for retaliatory action later on.

The earliest of the nuclear submarines, Polaris, carried more explosive power in their sixteen SLBMs than was used in all bombing throughout the Second World War. The SLBM range of 1,500 miles, fired from under the surface, gave them the ability to destroy all the major cities of the Soviet Union. They were relatively inaccurate (one or two miles perhaps) but this was unimportant as they were intended primarily for retaliation against people (second strike), not for attack against military bases.

A nuclear-powered submarine during sea trials

If that was all they could do, they would be a perfect second-strike weapon. Unfortunately to some extent they could also be used in a first strike. They could sneak close to military targets, such as harbours, well within their 1,500-mile range, and then score direct hits. It seemed possible that Polaris might take part in a first-strike attack. Although this was denied by America and Britain, the Russians saw Polaris as a first-strike threat and seven or eight years afterwards developed a similar nuclear submarine fleet – which America and Britain now see as a Russian threat.

Poseidon is an improvement on Polaris, with far more accurate and longer-range SLBMs. It is not clear why these improvements

Polaris missile firing

were necessary if Poseidon is intended merely for a second-strike strategy: Soviet cities were vulnerable already. So suspicions were intensified as Poseidon replaced Polaris.

Moreover yet another generation of nuclear submarines is being

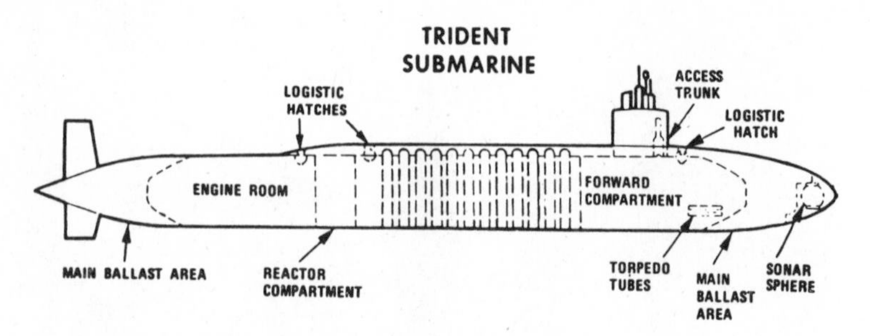

produced. This new American underwater long-range missile system (ULMS), using Trident submarines, has a range of 6,000 miles, an accuracy equivalent to the best of the present generation of ICBMs and will carry ten MIRVed warheads on each of its twenty-four SLBMs. A fleet of more than thirty Trident submarines is envisaged. The additional targets that will be reached by the Trident SLBMs (compared with those that can already be reached by Poseidon) are the Soviet missile sites in Kazakhstan. If the object of nuclear submarines is mere deterrence, there is no reason for adding extra *military* targets to the list. The new submarines may well be part of a planned development of a first-strike capability.

Anti-submarine warfare

Side by side with these developments come the inevitable counter-measures. Early proposals were for 'hunter-killer' nuclear submarines to tail the Polaris-type submarines. At a predetermined moment all the 'hunter-killer' submarines would destroy their Polaris quarries. Fortunately this proved impracticable – *very* fortunately, because the prospect of nuclear submarines chasing and dodging each other throughout the oceans was recognized as hazardous by all concerned.

The more 'promising' developments in anti-submarine warfare (ASW) are similar to those described earlier in relation to the electronic battlefield. The oceans will be sown with electronic devices to detect changes in temperature, noise, vibration and anything else that may indicate the presence of nuclear sub-

Above: *An ASROC missile firing during an anti-submarine warfare exercise*

Below: *An underwater nuclear explosion from an ASROC missile*

marines. These gadgets will be stationed permanently on the ocean bed or will float at pre-set depths, sending back signals for evaluation. The central control station would eventually have sufficient information to keep a continuous record of the

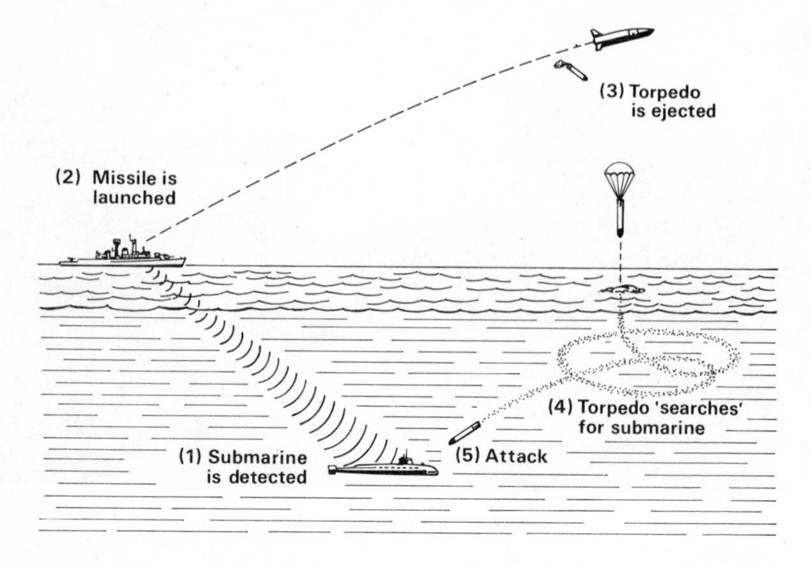

movements of all submarines. It would then be relatively simple to destroy all the enemy submarines by explosions underwater. Assuming a maximum of forty enemy nuclear submarines on patrol at any time, no more than forty nuclear warheads would be needed.

This programme is ambitious, but large amounts of money are being spent on it. The resources devoted to ASW and associated research now approach the sum expended on the space race. Success is unlikely to be achieved before 1985, but equally there is no reason to believe that the technical problems will not eventually be solved. The consequences could be serious. If the Russians feel that, with a few more years work, the USA could obtain a first-strike capability, they may panic and precipitate conflict to pre-empt that eventuality. Alternatively, and more probably, they may escalate their own military expenditure to counter the threat to their second-strike capability. So the arms race shows no sign of slowing down.

6. The nuclear arms race

I remember President Kennedy once stated . . . that the United States had the nuclear missile capacity to wipe out the Soviet Union two times over, while the Soviet Union had enough atomic weapons to wipe out the United States only once . . . When journalists asked me to comment . . . I said jokingly, 'Yes, I know what Kennedy claims, and he's quite right. But I'm not complaining . . . We're satisfied to be able to finish off the United States first time round. Once is quite enough. What good does it do to annihilate a country twice? We're not a bloodthirsty people.'

Nikita Khrushchev

'Minimum deterrence', according to former U S Defense Secretary Robert McNamara, needs about 400 thermonuclear warheads. With only moderate accuracy these could destroy about two thirds of Soviet industry and kill about sixty million people (excluding subsequent deaths from fallout, social disruption and starvation). Few countries would risk starting a nuclear war if this were the expected scale of retaliation.

With twice as many thermonuclear warheads (that is, 800) McNamara estimated that the industrial destruction would be around three quarters and the immediate death toll about eighty million. (This relatively small increase is because a lot of Soviet industry and population is widely dispersed in the countryside.) So, assuming that American policy stopped at minimum deterrence, about 400 thermonuclear bombs would be adequate whilst any more than 400 would be hardly worth the extra cost. Similar arguments apply to the Soviet Union.

Yet, by 1972, the Soviet Union and the USA each possessed far more SLBMs, ICBMs, aircraft and other missiles than either needed for minimum deterrence. Indeed, submarine-launched missiles alone provided sufficient warheads for 'minimum deterrence'. In addition both had over 1,000 ICBMs and the USA had several hundred bombers within striking range of the Soviet Union. 'I can go into my office and pick up the telephone and in twenty-five minutes seventy million people will be dead,' declared President Nixon at the height of his Watergate troubles.

Moreover missile numbers *underestimate* the degree of 'overkill' since most ICBMs now carry multi-warheads. At the time of the SALT agreements (May 1972) the number of deliverable nuclear *warheads* held by the USA and the USSR was about 5,700 and 2,100 respectively – both well above the 400 needed to satisfy the MAD (Mutually Assured Destruction) doctrine. If American and Soviet policies were simply MAD, then all but the SLBMs could be jettisoned. Their policies are more than MAD because the MIRVing of SLBMs and ICBMs and the incorporation of SRAMs on aircraft means that the number of deliverable warheads continues to increase.

In opposition to this trend it is sometimes argued that the yield (megaton power) of the average nuclear warhead is decreasing and, consequently, more warheads are needed to achieve the same destruction. This is simply not true: a scatter of small bombs spreads destruction more effectively than a single blockbuster. Moreover smaller nuclear warheads may be guided more accurately to their targets. This explains why the Polaris A3 missile, which originally had a single 1-megaton warhead, will have ten 50-kiloton MIRV warheads after current improvements. Although this drops the yield per missile from 1 to

0·5 megatons, the destructive capability is increased for all but very large cities.

Comparative effectiveness of different-sized missiles

	Number of targets destroyed	
Type of target	*One 10-megaton warhead*	*Ten 50-kiloton warheads*
Airfields	1·0	10
Hard-missile silos	1·0	1·2–1·7
Cities of 100,000	1·0	3·5
Cities of 500,000	1·0	0·7
Cities of 2,000,000	0·6	0·5

The effectiveness or 'kill probability' of a nuclear warhead depends upon its yield in megatons and its accuracy in nautical miles. The relative effectiveness of the Soviet and American missile forces are compared on the following pages; it will be seen that America has a huge advantage in kill probability, even though Russia has more missiles and greater total megatonnage. On 1975 figures America had more than fifteen and Russia more than five times the number of nuclear warheads necessary for minimum deterrence.

By 1980 the USA may have a 95-per-cent chance of destroying all Soviet missile silos, airfields and submarine bases in a first strike. But, assuming she did so and also destroyed a third of the Soviet nuclear submarines in their bases, this still would leave about 400 Soviet SLBMs available for minimum deterrence. So the United States, despite its enormous technological lead, has little immediate prospect of acquiring a first-strike capability and cannot use its power in any effective manner. Henry Kissinger expressed this frustration as 'The great paradox of the nuclear age. Power has never been greater; it has also never been less useful.'

*Comparison of Soviet and American missile effectiveness**

The effectiveness of a nuclear warhead depends upon its explosive power and the accuracy of its delivery system. More formally the lethality (k) of a nuclear warhead depends on its strength or 'yield' (y) and the accuracy of delivery (CEP). Accuracy is measured by 'circular error probability' (CEP) – the radius of a circle about the target in which 50 per cent of the bombs may be expected to fall (in nautical miles). So lethality is increased with powerful bombs (i.e. large y) and high accuracy (i.e. small CEP), the exact mathematical formula being, $k = y^{\frac{2}{3}}/(CEP)^2$.

The relative effectiveness of the Soviet and American armoury is therefore measured from the total lethality of all the deliverable nuclear warheads of the two countries – the sum of the products of k times N. The results *for missiles only* are set out below.

USA	*Missile numbers (n)*	*Warheads per missile*	*Warhead numbers (N)*	*Yield (megatons) (y)*	*Total megatons (N.y)*	*Accuracy (CEP)*	*Warhead lethality (k)*	*Total lethality (k.N)*
Minuteman 3	550	3	1,650	0·17	280	0·2	7·7	12,659
Minuteman 2	450	1	450	1·0	450	0·3	11·1	5,000
Titan	54	1	54	5·0	270	0·5	11·7	632
(Total ICBMs)	(1,054)		(2,154)		(1,000)			(18,291)
Poseidon	496	10	4,960	0·04	198	0·3	1·3	6,446
Polaris A-3	160	1	160	0·6	96	0·7	1·5	232
(Total SLBMs)	(656)		(5,120)		(294)			(6,678)
Total (all missiles)	1,710		7,274		1,294			24,969

	Missile numbers (n)	*Warheads per missile*	*Warhead numbers (N)*	*Yield (megatons) (y)*	*Total megatons (N.y)*	*Accuracy (CEP)*	*Warhead lethality (k)*	*Total lethality (k.N)*
USSR								
SS-9	288	1	288	25·0	7,200	0·7	17·4	5,025
SS-11	1,010	1	1,010	1·0	1,010	1·0	1·0	1,010
SS-13	60	1	60	1·0	60	0·7	2·0	122
SS-8	109	1	109	5·0	545	1·5	1·3	142
SS-7	100	1	100	5·0	500	2·0	0·7	73
(Total ICBMs)	(1,567)		(1,567)		(9,315)			(6,372)
SS-N-6	528	1	528	1·0	528	1·5	0·4	235
SS-N-8	180	1	180	1·0	180	0·8	1·6	281
(Total SLBMs)	(708)		(708)		(708)			(516)
Total (all missiles)	2,275		2,275		10,023			6,888

*Information from: Congressman Robert L. Leggatt, *US Armed Forces Journal International*, February 1975

So why continue?

Additional American military spending has been justified on the grounds that the Soviet Union has tested MIRVed missiles – a stage reached by the United States seven years earlier. Previously the Americans claimed to need MIRVs because of the (unsuccessful) Soviet ABM construction around Moscow in 1961 (though the American MIRV development actually started in 1958). In neither instance was there a real danger that the Soviet Union threatened the nuclear stalemate: none the less American countermeasures were taken and so the stalemate *was* threatened by the acceleration of the nuclear arms race.

Here is the nub. Every development by one side is interpreted, rightly or wrongly, as a threat by the other. Logically neither side need worry if they have enough to deter a nuclear attack. In this nuclear stalemate, a halt to all so-called improvements would not harm either side. In practice the arms race has a momentum of its own and has never slackened.

Whatever views are held about the politics and intentions of the Soviet Union, and the supposed level of her conventional armed forces, it must be admitted that the United States has led the nuclear arms race. Whether you consider the first nuclear bombs, ICBMs, MIRVs, nuclear submarines, SRAMs or ASW, the United States has been the pacemaker, usually with a lead of several years.

Yet this lead has not been decisive. The United States has never held a first-strike capability. At the same time American forces were too sophisticated and heavily armed for the fighting in Vietnam, which partly explains why small (that is, Hiroshima-strength) 'tactical' nuclear weapons have been developed for 'limited nuclear war'. Some tens of thousands of tactical nuclear weapons have been provided for the conventional forces deployed in Europe. The United States – in collaboration with her allies – has built up an impressive nuclear armoury, many times more powerful than that possessed by the Soviet Union and her allies.

Who is winning?

But is anyone really ahead? If both sides can destroy each other, neither has an advantage in real terms. There are three kinds of nuclear balance. There is the *destructive balance*, which stopped being meaningful once each side became able to wipe out the other a few times. (This was reached before 1960 when both had obtained more than 400 nuclear bombs.) Then there is the *second-strike balance* (minimum deterrence or mutually assured destruction). Once each side has reached the MAD stage (that is, the ability to deliver 400 or more nuclear bombs even after being attacked), this balance also stops being meaningful. Lastly there is the *first-strike balance* in which the USA has a huge lead which, fortunately, still falls short of the ability to achieve a successful first strike. If this ever were achieved, the second-strike capability of the Soviet Union will have been eroded and nuclear war could result.

Unfortunately there are always some people ready to urge that we need more arms to catch up with a mythical Soviet lead, and the publicity given to their views means that most people still think that new nuclear weapons are needed. A typical example, from *The Times* of 10 September 1973, is reproduced on page 104 and, although written by someone who took part in the decision to MIRV Polaris, Poseidon and Minuteman missiles, thus *decreasing* megatonnage, he complains of the fact that Russian missiles have more megatonnage than America's!

America's MIRVed ICBMs of the 1975 vintage were able on average to deliver three times as many warheads as the Russian ICBMs. As Henry Kissinger has succinctly commented: 'You are hit by warheads not missiles.' So the Soviet missile lead is worthless by comparison with the American warhead lead: the greater Soviet megatonnage merely showed that they were in fact ten years *behind* the Americans. In effect the Russians were still, in 1973, developing a massive second-strike capability for retaliation against big cities whilst the Americans were developing a first-strike capability.

The newest Soviet warhead, the SS-9, is 500 times more powerful than the United States' newest warhead, the Poseidon MIRV. If the Soviets choose to run a MIRV race, they could outpower the United States twenty times over. When the US MIRV their 4-megaton Poseidon, they split it into 50-kiloton warheads making a total of half a megaton for the missile. The Soviets could MIRV their 25-megaton SS-9 (of which they have 300) into ten 1-megaton warheads, making a total of 10 megatons per SS-9. To equate these two missiles would be dishonestly to conceal a Soviet advantage of 24,950,000 tons of explosive power.

The obvious riposte to the above would be to say that United States submarines prowl the seas carrying nuclear missiles which can hit any target with zero warning. But the true state of the game happens to be that the new Soviet ballistic missile submarine, which will carry 4,000-mile-range missiles, a much greater range than the best United States submarine-launched missiles, can be stationed in a stand-off posture opposite both United States coasts with atomic warheads targeted at every major city in the country . . .

Soviet nuclear superiority is clearly established by the SALT Agreements which President Nixon signed in Moscow with fanfare and formality in May 1972. These agreements proclaim to all the world that the Soviets are number one in military power and that the United States is now a poor second.

Walter Walker
Former Commander-in-Chief,
Allied Forces Northern Europe
(from *The Times*, September 1973)

Geography

A straight comparison of nuclear-submarine numbers is equally misleading. A realistic comparison has to allow for the number on patrol and this is determined primarily by the American nuclear submarines based at Holy Loch in Scotland and at Guam in the Pacific. These bases enable the American submarine fleet to be constantly within firing range of the Soviet Union. By contrast, Soviet submarines have to travel to their patrol area and this takes time. Thus, despite having a bigger fleet, the number of Soviet submarines on useful patrol is *less* than those of the Americans.

Geopolitics are also important in comparing missiles and aircraft. Whereas America has IRBM silos within range of the Soviet Union and can fly aircraft along Soviet borders, the USSR does not have such well-situated allies. So, quite apart from the advantage of greater accuracy, and their possession of SRAMs, the US superiority is even greater than indicated and appears likely to continue so for the foreseeable future.

Quality versus quantity

General Walker's claim that new Soviet submarines 'will carry 4,000-mile-range missiles' was not confirmed at the time of writing, but a 6,000-mile-range American SLBM is expected by 1978. It should be noted moreover that in the early 1970s most Soviet submarines were, in reality, merely submersible ships and needed to surface in order to fire their missiles. So they were far more vulnerable than the Western fleet.

These factors show that missile range on its own does not indicate the relative effectiveness of American and Soviet submarines. The military balance is complex, involving as it does missile numbers, accuracies, megatonnage, base locations and qualitative factors such as reliability and performance. Scare stories of a Soviet lead constantly appear to justify more improvements to

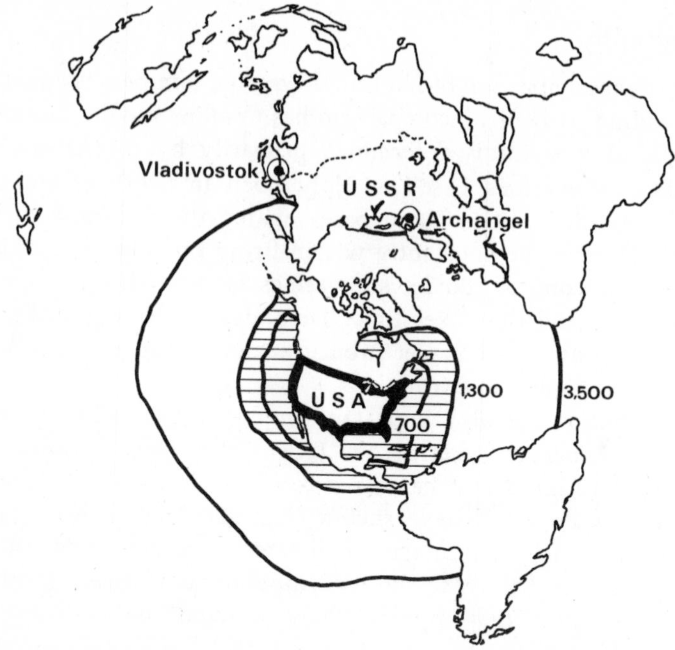

Sea area from which Soviet SLBMs could hit American targets within 200 miles of the American border. Their older missiles have a range of 700 nautical miles; their current missiles, 1,300 nautical miles; and a proposed missile, 3,500 nautical miles

Western weaponry but all independent assessments confirm Kennedy's boast of American superiority.

Conventional forces

Nuclear forces are not the only factor in the military balance. The nuclear superiority of the West is said to be matched by the superior conventional forces of the Warsaw Pact (the alliance between Russia and the East European countries). As Europe would be the theatre of operations, the argument with respect to front-line bases is reversed. The bulk of the Warsaw Pact forces are close to their presumed military objectives in Western Europe

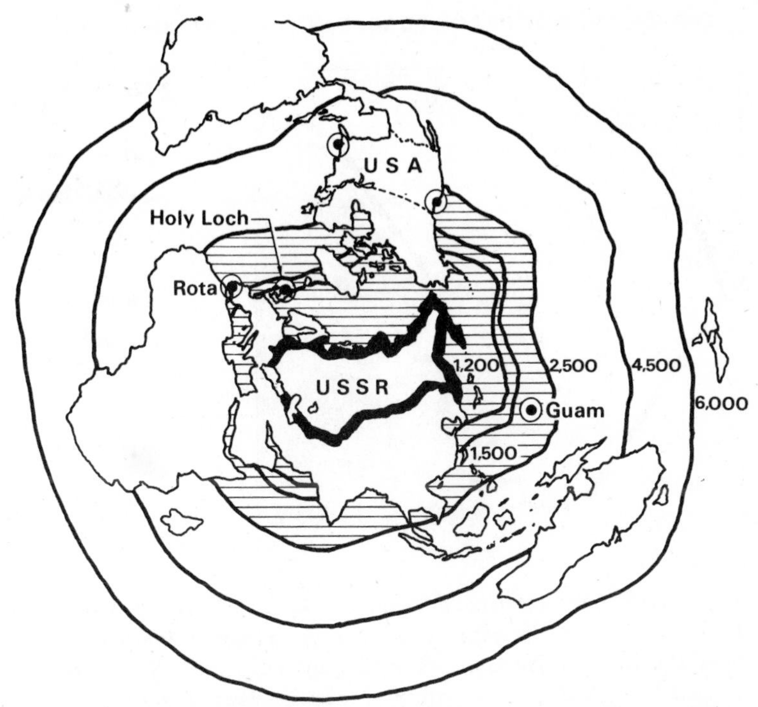

Sea areas from which American SLBMs could hit Soviet targets within 200 miles of the Soviet border. The range of the older Polaris missiles is 1,200 and 1,500 nautical miles; of the newer Polaris and Poseidon missiles, 2,500 nautical miles; and of the proposed Trident, 4,500 and 6,000 nautical miles

whereas most American forces are an ocean away. So the Soviet Union and her allies have stronger front-line bases for conventional warfare.

These arguments have validity but omit other aspects. One factor is the antagonism between the Soviet Union and China. A large proportion of the Soviet Union's forces is stationed along the Chinese border and only a small proportion could be used effectively in Europe. Although newspapers often quote figures which show Soviet military superiority, US Pentagon studies in

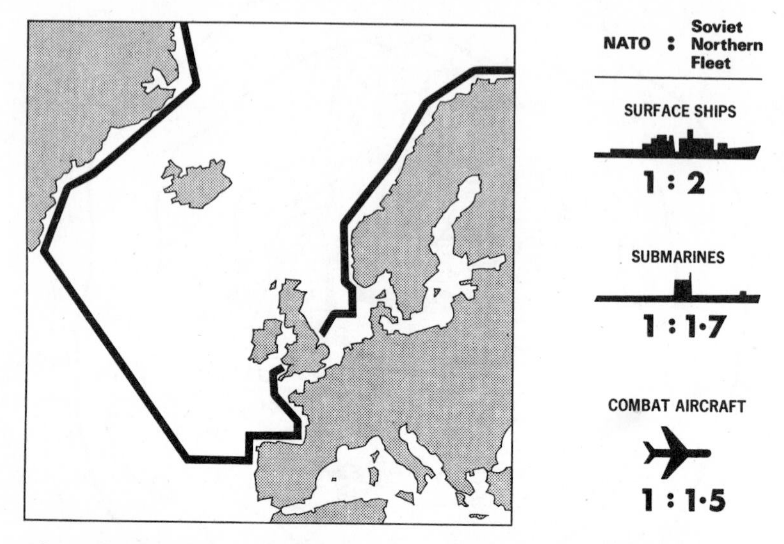

These illustrations, reproduced from the 1976 British Defence White Paper, make the Soviet military forces seem superior by omitting tactical nuclear weapons, anti-tank weapons, etc. (where NATO has an overwhelming lead) and by confining the comparisons to limited geographical areas

1962, 1968 and 1973 reached the conclusion that NATO conventional forces have been at least as strong as the Warsaw Pact in Europe throughout this period, even on a strict numerical basis.

According to James Meacham, Defence Correspondent of the *Economist*, writing in the October 1975 issue of *NATO Review:*

NATO today could probably fight the Warsaw Pact to a standstill in a conventional war in Central Europe. Its forces are large enough, although not as large as they should be; its equipment is better, although not as good as it should be for the money that is spent on it; and its disposition is at least adequate, if not ideal . . . Although the Warsaw Pact's numerical superiority is clear, it is by no means overwhelming. If it should succeed in concentrating a superior force, say 3 or 4 to 1,

THE MILITARY BALANCE ON NATO'S CENTRAL FRONT (READY FORCES)

	NATO	Warsaw Pact	NATO: Warsaw Pact
TOTAL SOLDIERS			1:1·3
SOLDIERS IN FIGHTING UNITS			1:1·4
MAIN BATTLE TANKS			1:2·7
FIELD GUNS			1:2·5
TACTICAL AIRCRAFT			1:2·3

in a small area, it could very likely achieve breakthrough. But presumably NATO commanders would be doing something to redress the balance. NATO's equipment is, by and large, a lot better than the Warsaw Pact's.

The fact that the Warsaw Pact has almost twice the number of *divisions* as NATO does not in itself mean that they are stronger. Each Warsaw Pact division has only about *half the soldiers* of a NATO division and is less well equipped. NATO divisions are manned overwhelmingly by regular troops and possess at least 6,000 tactical nuclear weapons; by contrast most Warsaw Pact soldiers are conscripts and they have not usually been entrusted with such weapons.

NATO superiority in conventional weaponry was confirmed by former Head of Defence Intelligence, General Daniel Graham, when talking about the standard Russian battle tank, the T-62:

The T-62 is really a T-54 tank (first manufactured in 1948) that has been modified a little here and a little there. It has the same engine in it that the Soviets had in their tanks in World War II. There are some drawbacks to that. It isn't a powerful enough engine. Our tank does outrange their tank. I have been in a T-62 and it has a very cramped turret, and you have to be a left-handed midget because you have to load the darn thing from the wrong side of the breech. And you have to be about my size. If they run out of left-handed midgets in the Soviet Union, they are going to be in big trouble with the T-62.

Two types of Soviet rocket

Military balance

The foregoing has not been intended as an apologia for the level of Soviet conventional forces. The purpose has been to show that claims of massive Soviet superiority are quite unfounded and to show that neither side has a clear military advantage in nuclear or conventional forces. Neither side dare risk a conventional war; if they did, this could very easily escalate into a nuclear war which would destroy both. None the less the arms race has been fuelled by claims that the other side had an overwhelming military lead – particularly evident in the case of the United States, where arguments are conducted in public. For example, before 1960 Senator J. F. Kennedy gained much support in his election campaign by blaming the Republicans for allowing the Soviet Union an enormous lead in missiles. After he became President, and after a big increase in US missile expenditure, it was 'discovered' that the 'missile gap' did not exist.

Similarly MIRV was developed because of a mythical threat of a Soviet ABM and, in 1969, the US Congress sanctioned expenditure on the Trident submarines and the B-1 bomber in response to an alleged Soviet MIRV development. Two years later the photographic evidence for Soviet MIRVs was admitted officially to be worthless. Unfortunately many of the predictions of Soviet intentions are self-fulfilling since the decision to step up US arms expenditure naturally stimulates the Soviet Union to do the same.

The Soviet Union has had valid reasons for believing that America might be ahead and perhaps cannot be blamed for staying in the race. Nonetheless in certain respects they too have undertaken unjustified military developments. For example, the abortive attempt to build ABM defences around Moscow provided a useful post-justification for the US MIRV developments. But this is the only instance of a past Soviet initiative that could have been honestly misinterpreted as an attempt to obtain first-strike capability.

A more serious and recent development is believed to have

begun in 1974 with the testing of Soviet MIRVs. As argued earlier, these are unambiguous first-strike weapons and the American initiative to develop MIRV must be deplored. In this case Soviet military strategists appear to have successfully argued for parity – they want the same opportunity to start a nuclear war. It would have been more acceptable had they decided to make the Soviet nuclear submarine fleet more invulnerable or provided greater missile protection: this would discourage an American-inspired nuclear war for less cost and risk.

One of the great paradoxes of the 1970s has been this acceleration of the nuclear arms race in a period of detente between the superpowers. There is a much greater appreciation of the dangers of nuclear war and of the spread of nuclear weapons, but this has not been matched by moves to halt, let alone reverse, the construction of new weapons. All previous arms races in history have ended in war. If the nuclear arms race continues, sooner or later, by accident or design, there will be a nuclear war.

The Dynamics of the Arms Race

Robert S. McNamara

The United States must not and will not permit itself ever to get into a position in which another nation, or combination of nations, would possess a first-strike capability against it. Such a position not only would constitute an intolerable threat to our security, but it obviously would remove our ability to deter nuclear aggression.

We are not in that position today, and there is no foreseeable danger of our ever getting into that position . . . Our alert forces alone carry more than 2,200 weapons, each averaging more than the explosive equivalent of 1 megaton of TNT. Four hundred of these delivered on the Soviet Union would be sufficient to destroy over one third of her population and one half of her industry. All these flexible and highly reliable forces are equipped with devices that ensure their penetration of Soviet defenses . . .

The most frequent question that arises is whether or not the United States possesses nuclear superiority over the Soviet Union. The answer is that we do . . . the most meaningful and realistic measurement of nuclear capability is the number of separate warheads that can be delivered accurately on individual high-priority targets with sufficient power to destroy them . . .

One point should be made quite clear, however: our current numerical superiority over the Soviet Union in reliable, accurate and effective warheads is both greater than we had originally planned and more than we require . . .

How this came about is a significant illustration of the intrinsic dynamics of the nuclear arms race.

In 1961 when I became Secretary of Defense, the Soviet Union had a very small operational arsenal of intercontinental missiles. However, it did possess the technological and industrial capacity to enlarge that arsenal very substantially over the succeeding several years. We had no evidence that the Soviets did plan, in fact, fully to use that capability. But, as I have pointed out, a strategic planner must be conservative in his calculations; that is, he must prepare for the worst plausible case and not be content to hope and prepare merely for the most probable.

Since we could not be certain of Soviet intentions, since we could not be sure that they would not undertake a massive build-up, we had to insure against such an eventuality by undertaking a major buildup of our own Minuteman and Polaris forces. Thus, in the course of hedging against what was then only a theoretically possible Soviet buildup, we took decisions which have resulted in our current superiority in numbers of warheads and deliverable megatons. But the blunt fact remains that, if we had had more accurate information about planned Soviet strategic forces, we simply would not have needed to build as large a nuclear arsenal as we have today . . .

In recent years the Soviets have substantially increased their offensive forces. We have been watching and evaluating this very carefully, of course; clearly the Soviet buildup is in part a reaction to our own buildup since the beginning of the 1960s. Soviet strategic planners undoubtedly reasoned that, if our build-up were to continue at its accelerated pace, we might conceivably reach in time a credible first-strike capability against the Soviet Union.

(from *The Essence of Security*, 1968)

7. How war might start

The danger of outbreak of war by accident . . . grows as modern weapons become more complex, command and control difficulties increase, and the premium is on ever-faster reaction.

Dean Rusk,
US Secretary of State, 1962

It must be well understood that if Russia were to launch a major attack, even with conventional weapons only, the West would have to hit back with strategic nuclear weapons.

1958 British Defence White Paper

Many people think that a nuclear war is quite likely to start by accident. Preparations for quick retaliation are so extensive that a mistake could set off a train of events that could end with a nuclear holocaust.

Faulty electronics

NATO has radar and scanning systems to detect missile launches, aircraft flights, submarine movements and any other unusual events which might herald a surprise attack. The Soviet Union probably has something similar. Each of these 'early-warning' systems depends upon complex and sophisticated electronic equipment which constantly scans areas of many thousands of square miles. Just as television sets and computers break down from time to time, so do these. On average each instrument gives a false signal about once every three months.

In 1961 a mistaken interpretation by America's early-warning system led the US strategic air force to fly off to bomb Russia. After two hours flying the aircraft were recalled as, by then, it had been discovered that the original signal was merely a moon echo. If the same mistake happened today, ICBMs could land in Moscow within an hour, long before the recall signal could be sent.

On another occasion atmospheric disturbances completely disrupted the NATO early-warning system and it was thought that the Russians might have exploded a nuclear bomb to deliberately black it out. A flight of geese in a formation akin to that of a fighter bomber has been another source of confusion. Any one of these or similar errors could have led to a nuclear war.

'How was I to know our formation flying would show up on their early-warning system?'

Early-warning systems use a variety of techniques, and a vast amount of information is collected. Ground-radar systems, similar to those used in the Second World War, detect oncoming aeroplanes and missiles; over-the-horizon (OTH) stations monitor radio signals bounced off the ionosphere to give advance indication of missile launches (the ionosphere is disturbed by rocket exhausts); and satellites keep a constant watch over the world's surface for unusual events of any kind. With so much data available, the process of deciding whether an event is unusual or dangerous has to be assigned to special electronic equipment – people would take too long over this task.

As early-warning systems become more sophisticated and swifter counter-attacks are envisaged, there will be less opportunity for second thoughts if an attack is started in error. In the near future it will be possible to launch a counter-attack by electronic signals rather than human intervention. Early-warning systems could be coupled directly to missile-firing systems, and so missiles launched automatically on receipt of a warning signal. Then, in the event of an error, there would be no possibility of recall.

People are a good safeguard against faulty equipment. At present the early-warning systems are able to *instruct* people to fire missiles, but human beings are still responsible for the ultimate decision. And, to safeguard against a single person taking a rash step, missile-firing systems usually require two or more keys to be turned simultaneously at separate locations.

Another common safeguard at the moment is an '*electronic key*' which has to be received by radio before a human operator can launch the missiles. However, if the missiles are being used in retaliation, radio messages might be drowned by the interference from nuclear explosions. So it is likely that ways have been devised to get round these remote-control electronic keys.

Remote-control electronic safeguards have their own dangers. On one occasion an H-bomb plane had its electronic key activated by a tune from a Spanish 'pop' station and was thus primed for action. Despite all precautions, there is no certainty that an accidental missile firing will not occur one day.

Collisions

There have been at least thirteen accidents involving planes carrying nuclear bombs and, on one occasion, a B52 bomber crashed over South Carolina with a 10-megaton bomb on board. The bomb was equipped with five interlocking safety devices to prevent an accidental explosion but, on recovery, four of the five safety devices were found to have been triggered by the fall. Had the bomb exploded, it could have been interpreted as a surprise Russian attack and America might have 'counter-attacked'.

PALOMARES: the dangers of nuclear accidents were well illustrated when a B-52 bomber collided with a tanker aircraft during a mid-air refuelling operation over the Spanish village of Palomares on 17 January 1966. The photographs on this page show a typical refuelling operation and debris from this collision

*PALOMARES: following the collision (see page 119) three 10-megaton H-bombs fell on the land around Palomares and a fourth into the sea. Those that fell on land were recovered quickly though one had been damaged, causing radioactive contamination nearby. Fifteen US warships and two submarines searched for many weeks before the fourth bomb was recovered. The photographs show (*above*) villagers outside their home near the spot where one of the bombs fell; (*below*) checks against radioactive contamination of farm livestock; (*top right*) US servicemen of the decontamination team; (*centre right*) US soldiers hosing down soil in case of radioactivity; and (*bottom right*) on 19 March thousands of barrels of contaminated soil about to be loaded for transportation to South Carolina, USA, for disposal*

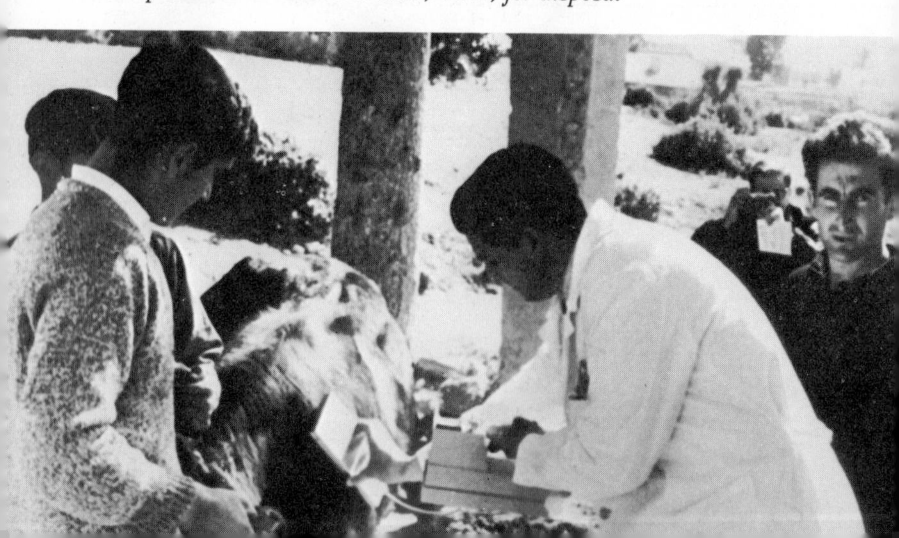

Britain's nuclear submarines have been involved in several minor collisions. One surfaced under a fishing boat in the middle of the Irish Sea. On another occasion, two of the submarines contrived to hit each other! In 1976 the U S House of Representatives Intelligence Committee learnt that U S nuclear submarines on patrols in Soviet waters had collided with 'hostile vessels' nine times in the previous sixteen years. The consequences of a major collision would not be funny. An accident to any bomb carrier or store could lead to a misunderstanding that might precipitate nuclear war.

Two views inside nuclear submarines

People

There is also a risk that the people in charge of nuclear weapons may make a mistake or go berserk. The type of person who is put in charge of a missile silo or goes to sea in a Polaris submarine is carefully chosen to be cool in emergencies and convinced of the rightness in some circumstances of mass destruction.

In an interview with Jonathan Steele of the *Guardian* (reported on 9 October 1975), one young officer of the US base at Omaha, Nebraska, put it this way: 'We have two tasks. The first is not to let people go off their rockers. That's the negative side. The positive one is to ensure that people act without moral compunction.'

Imagine being cooped up in a submarine for three months on end, never seeing daylight and sleeping next to weapons of

mass destruction. Such conditions are not normal and they can create special psychiatric problems. Similarly those who man missile silos go down into the bowels of the earth each day to check missiles whose purpose is to kill thousands of people at the press of a button. These men undergo regular psychiatric checks and often become disturbed mentally.*

To overcome the danger of men going berserk, crews have been supplied with pistols and have been given instructions to shoot anyone who appears likely to fire missiles without proper authorization. This is a rational precaution against the possibility of madness but it cannot help but contribute to the abnormal atmosphere. In addition to everything else that might cause worry, each man knows that his companion has a loaded pistol which he has a right and duty to use, should he believe (or say that he believes) his colleague has gone mad.

Nor is it only the people in charge of the missiles and submarines that could cause an inadvertent nuclear explosion. Thousands of tactical nuclear weapons are scattered around Europe under the control of field commanders. Although their working conditions are not as claustrophobic as those of the submarine and missile silo crews, they also can suffer mental disorders. In 1972 a homesick US pilot climbed into a bomber aircraft at a US H-bomb base in East Anglia, flew off and crashed in the English Channel whilst being 'pursued' by other American airforce planes.

One possibility that is often overlooked is that the generals might not wait for authorization to use the weapons under their control. Lord (formerly General) Montgomery wrote in the *Royal United Services Institute Journal*, November 1956:

*A New York psychiatrist, Dr Jonathan Serxner, has investigated the mental state of Polaris submarine crews. Despite lectures, classes, cinema shows and other entertainments, religious services and a library, he found feuds and various minor psychiatric disturbances (about one in twenty of the men needed treatment). There was a chief petty officer who, after five weeks at sea, had delusions of persecution and heard voices. He was given heavy sedation and later transferred from submarine service.

Lord Montgomery of Alamein

. . . if we are attacked, we use nuclear weapons in our defence. That is agreed; the only proviso is that the politicians have to be asked first. That might be a bit awkward, of course, and personally I would use the weapon first and ask afterwards.

Then there are statesmen who go berserk. In 1949, two months after his retirement, former US Secretary of Defense James V. Forrestall committed suicide by jumping from a sixteenth-storey balcony. He had become so convinced of the Communist 'threat' that when a fire engine disturbed his sleep he ran out in his pyjamas screaming that the Russians were coming. The most serious aspect of his mental illness was that many Defense Department officials and journalists accepted his anti-Soviet hallucinations whilst he was still in office.

James Forrestall (left)

Confidence-building

The danger of war by accident, miscalculation, insanity or simple human error is sufficiently serious for America and Russia to have agreed on exceptional measures to try to prevent these eventualities. The Hotline Agreement signed in 1963, with supplements in 1971, means that the leaders of the two nations can now quickly confer. This bomb-proof phone line is supposed to prevent war by misunderstanding. In the event of an accident or an international crisis it enables the leaders of the two superpowers to talk to each other. If it is all a misunderstanding they quickly reassure each other and unintended full-scale war can be avoided.

But the Hotline cannot inspire complete confidence. Suppose the plane that crashed in South Carolina had caused a nuclear explosion. The American President might not know exactly what had happened and might suspect that this had been an attack from the Soviet Union. He would use the Hotline to ask whether this was the case and the Soviet leader would say that his country was not responsible. But the American President would have expected that reply anyway since a country planning a surprise attack would not use the Hotline to say 'yes, but it's a secret'! So, even with the Hotline, suspicions could lead a superpower chief to presume that an attack was in progress.

Thus the Hotline Agreement is no guarantee against war by accident. There needs to be mutual trust and confidence between the leaders. So constant contacts outside times of crisis are very important. If the leaders know each other personally, they may be less likely to believe that the other is capable of duplicity.

On non-vital matters there is now considerable exchange of information. At the Helsinki conference in 1975 it was agreed that each side would warn the other of all military manoeuvres. Now, when there are to be large troop movements in Eastern Europe, the West knows in advance that this is to happen as a routine manoeuvre and does not fear that it is a prelude to a Soviet attack. In the same way tests of missile firings are announced beforehand to avoid being mistaken for the beginning of a nuclear first strike. These exchanges of information help to build confidence in each other's intentions.

In addition to measures which depend upon the voluntary supply of information, activities can be checked unilaterally. Atmospheric nuclear explosions can be detected by satellites which circle the earth testing for radioactivity. Military stations monitor signals from the ionosphere indicating when missiles have been launched. So the American President, at the time of the South Carolina crash, could have been told immediately that there was no indication of a recent Soviet launch.

The straightforward way to prevent an accidental nuclear war is to abolish all nuclear weapons. But, failing actual disarmament, weapons have been developed which are less likely to lead to accidents. For example, the old liquid-fuelled rockets were more likely to blow up on their launch pads than the modern solid-fuelled rockets. No one wants to see a nuclear accident lead on to the holocaust, and very deliberate measures are taken to avoid this eventuality. Nevertheless, with perhaps forty or fifty thousand nuclear devices in various sites around the world, the possibility of accidental nuclear explosions cannot be ignored.

Limited nuclear war

The borderline between rational and irrational behaviour is never more blurred than when the topic of 'limited nuclear war' is discussed. This idea supposes that countries will fight with 'small' nuclear weapons over 'small battlefields' (that is, drop Hiroshima-strength bombs all over Europe) but will stop short of all-out nuclear war. It has been suggested as a humane alternative to the inflexible massive nuclear retaliation advocated, for example, in the 1958 British Defence White Paper. But it is dangerous to believe *any* nuclear war will not lead to universal destruction, for the first use of nuclear weapons then becomes more acceptable.

This theory forms the basis for official NATO strategy in the event of a European war and largely owes its adoption to former British Defence Minister, Denis Healey. In the event of our appearing to be losing a conventional European war, NATO will drop 'nukes' (big nuclear bombs) on cities such as Prague and Warsaw and use 'mini-nukes' (small nuclear bombs) on the battlefields. The obliteration of 'less important' targets will convince the Russians that we are serious so – the theory goes – they will stop fighting.

The difficulty is that the Russians may then decide to destroy 'less important' cities like London, Manchester and Glasgow to stop us fighting. What do we do then? In the words of Morton Halperin, formerly US Deputy Assistant Secretary of Defense, 'The NATO doctrine is that we will fight with conventional forces until we are losing, then we will fight with tactical nuclear weapons until we are losing, and then we will blow up the world.'

If the horror of nuclear war is not sufficient to prevent hostilities breaking out in the first place, is it likely that statesmen and generals will suddenly become cool and rational during a war? Lord Mountbatten has commented:

> During my six years on the NATO Military Committee I never missed an opportunity of saying, loud and clear, that the actual use of tactical nuclear weapons could only end in escalation to total global nuclear destruction, and for that reason no one in their senses would contemplate their use.

If one accepts Lord Mountbatten's view, it means that either the NATO strategy is a sham and the so-called tactical nuclear weapons are a gigantic bluff or, alternatively, that the NATO strategy is serious and those in charge are not 'in their senses'. Either way it is clear that conventional hostilities in Europe might easily be a prelude to an all-out nuclear war.

The 'flexible' response strategy is worse in some ways than the 1958 policy of massive retaliation for, by making nuclear war apparently more acceptable, it may bring forward the day on which nuclear weapons are first used. It also allows NATO to 'increase its options and to be able to counter aggression at any level by an appropriate choice of responses, leaving the enemy in doubt as to which response would be selected'.* The 1958 strategy of massive retaliation, by contrast, at least had the virtue that it deterred *all* hostilities. The new strategy justifies the development of all kinds of conventional armaments whilst at the same time doing nothing to remove the risk of an ultimate nuclear conflict.

Moreover one man's limited nuclear war is another man's

*NATO Handbook, 1975.

A tactical nuclear weapon, the French Pluton ground-to-air missile system might be used in a limited nuclear war. Its atomic charge is about 20 kilotons, with a range of 60 miles when mounted on a tank. The West Germans have offered France facilities to station these missiles near to their East German frontier

holocaust. The use of even 10 per cent of the 7,000 tactical nuclear weapons in Europe would destroy the entire region where the nuclear exchanges occurred. Nor is Europe the only possible flash-point for a nuclear war. In October 1973 President Nixon put all US forces, including those based in Britain, on a world-wide nuclear alert, the occasion being another round in the Arab–Israeli conflict. So a nuclear war need not necessarily arise only from a direct Soviet–American misunderstanding:

a dispute elsewhere in the world could trigger the sequence of events.

Whilst neither of the superpowers has a first-strike capability, no one *in their senses* will risk an all-out nuclear war. Unfortunately this is no guarantee against the possibility of war. For true security the world needs nuclear disarmament.

8. Arms control

Eminent authorities declare that both the US and the Soviet Union now possess nuclear stockpiles large enough to exterminate mankind three or four – some say ten – times over. What is the point of limiting arsenals like that? The only practical effect would be to give an air of legitimacy to the continued possession of an armoury of death which, on every ground of morality and common sense, ought to be destroyed.

Philip Noel-Baker,
Nobel Peace Prizewinner

With the sole exception of the Biological Weapons Convention, there have been *no* disarmament agreements since 1945, nor are any in sight. The agreements that have been reached merely limit areas in which arms may be used or the numbers of weapons that may be produced. Ironically, they often have the effect of accelerating the arms race in areas not covered by the agreements.

The 1972 SALT-1 agreement shows the weakness of a partial measure. It was agreed to limit the number of missiles in underground silos and nuclear submarines but not to halt 'qualitative improvements' to the missiles. But, before the 1972 agreement, America was MIRVing these missiles (having concluded that this was a cheaper and more effective way of adding to her nuclear armoury). She did not intend (or have the immediate ability) to build new missiles anyway. Secretary of State

Henry Kissinger, in his briefing to the US Congress, explained:

For various reasons during the 1960s the United States had, as you know, made the strategic decision to terminate its building programs in major offensive systems and to rely instead on qualitative improvements.

By 1969, therefore, we had no active or planned programmes for deploying additional ICBMs, submarine-launched ballistic missiles or bombers. The Soviet Union, on the other hand, had dynamic and accelerated deployment programs in both land-based and sea-based missiles.

So the purpose of an arms control agreement may well be to secure a temporary military advantage under the guise of halting the nuclear arms race. In this sense arms control does not necessarily indicate a step towards disarmament. President Nixon made this clear at his Press Conference on the SALT-1 agreement:

. . . the offensive limitation is one that is particularly in our interest because it covers arms where the Soviet Union has ongoing programmes, which will be limited in this five-year period, and in which we have no ongoing programmes.

A further problem with arms control treaties is that they often accelerate the arms race during the negotiating period: more arms are made beforehand as 'bargaining chips'. At the same press conference President Nixon justified the previous expenditure on ABM:

I can say to the members of the Press here that had we not had an ABM program in being there would be no SALT agreement today because there would be no incentive for the Soviet Union to stop us from doing something that we were doing; and, thereby, agree to stop something they were doing.

So there are usually two results of partial arms control measures: frenzied competition in the shortly-to-be-controlled weapons just before the agreement; and even more frenzied competition in the uncontrolled weapons afterwards.

New chips for SALT
Art Buchwald

While the rest of the country is fast asleep, there are men in Washington working on new defense weapons that will protect us from any enemy foolish enough to test our will.

One of them is Kipness, who lives down the street. The other day at an outdoor barbecue, Kipness told me about a new weapons system which he was involved with which would make all other systems obsolete.

It was called WANGO, which stands for Walter, Arthur, Neil, George and Oscar.

Kipness said, 'I don't believe I'm talking out of school because we're going up to the Hill in a few days to ask for fifteen billion dollars to get it off the drawing board.'

'What is it?' I asked.

'Well, as you know we now have submarines that can fire ten multiple missiles at one time. WANGO is a system that can fire ten submarines from a missile at the same time.'

'That's a lot of submarines,' I said, 'But what good is it to fire submarines from the air at the enemy?'

'It's not good,' Kipness said, 'except that it's a chip in the SALT talk poker game.'

'I'm not too sure what the SALT talk poker game is all about.'

'It's quite simple. When you negotiate with the Russians, you have to have a certain amount of chips. You say to them, "If you give up Mirving, we'll give up Marving". Our chip is the MARV and their chip is the MIRV.' . . .

'I guess fifteen billion dollars isn't too much to pay for a chip like WANGO.'

'Fifteen billion dollars is just to find out if it will work. We'll need forty billion dollars to put it into production. But it's a good investment, because if it works we can also sell it to the Shah of Iran.'

'And if it doesn't work?'

'We'll sell it to the Shah anyway. The important thing when talking with the Soviets is for us to keep coming up with new weapons systems so they'll know we're serious about trying to stop the arms race.'

'And then they'll come up with new systems to show they're just as serious about disarmament.'

'Right. The more weapons we can both develop, the better chance we have of coming to the SALT agreement. If we let them know we have WANGO, they may be willing to stop making IVAN.'

'What's IVAN?'

'It stands for Ilitch, Victor, Anatole and Nathan.'

(from the *International Herald Tribune*)

The frequency of nuclear tests between 1951 and 1973. Note the extra large number just before the Partial Test Ban Treaty (PTBT) was agreed in 1963

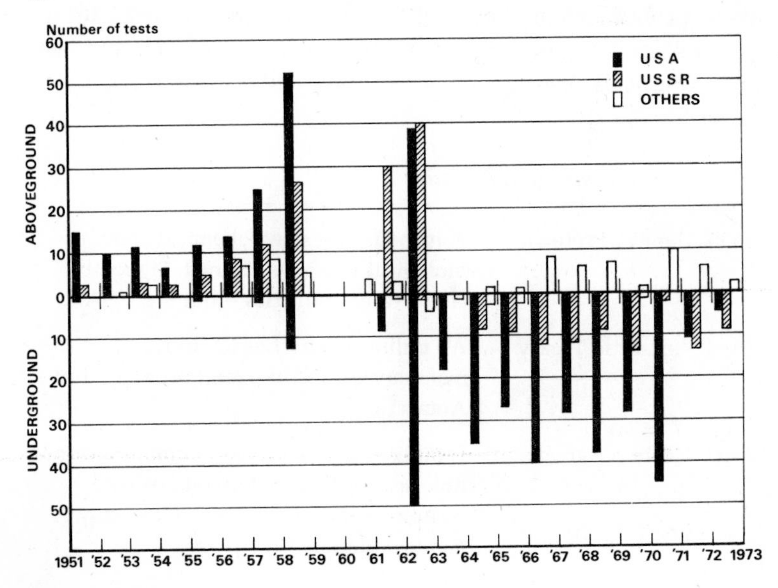

Historically arms control measures have never halted an arms race. This is because, by their very nature, they are 'deals' between competitors to resolve temporary problems: they do not tackle the root causes of the conflict. In the case of the PTBT it was agreed to halt radioactive pollution of the atmosphere – not the nuclear arms race. In the case of the SALT-1 agreements military and economic needs coincided with limitations on the numbers of ICBMs and SLBMs.

Moreover arms control agreements can help countries secure an advantage over their potential rivals. When the PTBT was signed by the USA, USSR and UK, these countries had already conducted a large number of nuclear tests in the atmosphere. By contrast France and China were not as advanced and were not ready or able to carry out all their tests below ground. The PTBT seemed to France and China to be a device to keep the three leading nuclear powers permanently ahead.

So France and China refused to sign the PTBT and have suffered world-wide unpopularity by conducting atmospheric nuclear tests, whereas the leading nuclear powers received little protest when they continued their nuclear tests underground, at a far higher rate than France and China, and with the American testing rate 40 per cent *above* their pre-PTBT level.

International arms control treaties

1925	Geneva Protocol	Poisonous gases and chemical and biological weapons banned. Signed by eighty-four countries – but *not* USA.
1959	Antarctic Treaty	All military activities (including manoeuvres, testing, etc.) prohibited in Antarctica.
1963	Hotline Agreement	Establishment of a direct communications link between the national command centres of the two powers. (Two supplements added in 1971.)

1963	Partial Test Ban Treaty (PTBT)	All nuclear tests prohibited except those conducted underground. Signed by USA, USSR and UK and over 100 other countries – but *not* France and China.
1967	Outer Space Treaty	Outer space, including the moon, not to be 'appropriated' by any country; and no nuclear weapons to be put on the moon or in orbit around the earth.
1967 and 1968	Treaty for the Prohibition of Nuclear Weapons in Latin America (Treaty of Tlatelolco)	Part 1: Latin American countries agree to being a nuclear-free zone. *Not* ratified by Argentina. Part 2: Nuclear powers recognize and agree to be bound by the Treaty. *Not* signed by USSR.
1968	Non-Proliferation Treaty (NPT)	Nations without nuclear weapons to take no steps to procure them; and nations with nuclear weapons not to help any non-nuclear nation to obtain them. Signed by USA, USSR, UK and over eighty other countries – but *not* France, China, Cuba, Israel, India, Pakistan, Brazil, Argentina or South Africa.
1971	Sea-bed Arms Control Treaty	The placing of weapons of mass destruction on the sea-bed prohibited. *Not* signed by France or China.
1972	Biological Warfare Convention	All biological weapons that exist to be destroyed; and no more such weapons to be manufactured. *Not* signed by France, China or India.
1972	Strategic Arms Limitation Talks (SALT), Interim Agreement	Specific limitations on the numbers of ABMs, intercontinental land-based missiles and missiles launched from US and Soviet submarines.
1974	Threshold Agreement	USA and USSR agree not to test nuclear weapons with a yield of more than 150 kilotons (to come into force in 1976).

The same issues are involved in the 1974 USA/USSR 'threshold limitation' of nuclear tests to a ceiling of 150 kilotons. The leading nuclear powers have conducted many tests above 150 kilotons and no longer need big tests. All foreseeable developments are in miniaturization. France, China and India are hardly likely to accede to such a threshold agreement before they too have reached this stage.

If all nuclear tests had been banned in 1963, this would have meant that the three leading nuclear powers were *genuinely* forgoing the development of improved nuclear arms. There is a distinct possibility that the Comprehensive Test Ban Treaty (CTBT), when it is eventually agreed, will be too late to halt all possible developments of all possible nuclear bombs for the USA and USSR. In that event it is likely that the other nuclear powers will again refuse to participate, on the grounds that the CTBT will discriminate in favour of the leading nuclear powers.

The failing of the treaties so far mentioned is that they are not all-embracing. The same applies to the 'geographic treaties' (Latin America, Antarctica, Outer Space and the Sea-bed). These are almost irrelevant. Nobel Peace Prizewinner, Philip Noel-Baker, commented that 'while disarming Antarctica, we put 7,000 nuclear weapons in Europe; we should have disarmed Europe and put those weapons in Antarctica.'

Admirable as it is to have any region nuclear-free, the effect of these limitations has been to divert public attention from the intensified competition elsewhere. Disarmament will not be accomplished through more and more arms control measures of this nature, useful as they may appear. Paradoxically, comprehensive disarmament may be easier to implement than arms control, for it involves the total destruction of familiar weapons rather than partial limitations over unfamiliar objects. Moreover suspicions that continue with arms control are allayed as complete disarmament proceeds. All sides to a disarmament agreement will take good care to verify that the others honour the treaty: with arms control the incentive is to break the treaty on the assumption that other countries are doing the same.

Verification

Even though the SALT-1 agreements and the Biological Weapons Convention were agreed without special provisions for verification, it is often claimed that other treaties are impracticable because of the risk of cheating.

The popular form of the argument claims that arms control and disarmament are impracticable because the Soviet Union will not accept inspection in her territory. The Soviet Union is indeed extraordinarily sensitive on this matter, especially when you consider that most of her 'secrets' are known to the West through the use of satellite and other spy techniques. However, on-site inspection has not been considered necessary for *any* of the arms control agreements so far mentioned and there is reason to believe that this issue will not be relevant for any future possible treaties either.

Take the problem of detecting underground nuclear tests. The PTBT banned atmospheric nuclear tests only, because underground nuclear explosions were said to be undetectable. Have a look at the photograph on the following page of an underground nuclear test. It would have been easily seen from a satellite. Moreover before the actual explosion, earth-moving and other activity would have been noticeable as preparations went ahead. If the explosion had been conducted farther underground, to avoid the cave-in and collapse, then, correspondingly, a truly massive excavation would need to have taken place beforehand. So clandestine underground nuclear tests *can* be seen by satellite observation.

Nor is that all. Underground nuclear tests can be detected by the same seismic observation stations that are used to monitor earthquakes. In 1963 negotiations for a comprehensive test ban treaty ended with America and Britain insisting on seven annual on-site inspections to check against Russia cheating whilst the

A subsidence crater caused by an underground, intermediate-yield atomic explosion. It left a crater 125 feet deep and 425 feet in width, and a chimney which reached the surface and caused this visible depression

Russians would only agree to three. The Russian view that seismic detection was sufficiently sensitive to detect underground explosions above 10 kilotons without on-site inspection is now generally agreed. If a threshold agreement at, say, 20 kilotons had been signed in 1963, the world would have been spared much of the succeeding arms race.

There was also the suggestion that 'black box' monitoring stations be installed in the Soviet Union and the USA so that seismographic records could be investigated without any need for permanent on-site inspectors. If the Americans were truly concerned with the Russians cheating, this proposal should have been acceptable. If the Russians were truly concerned with the danger of American spies, black box records would have allayed these fears. As it transpired, both Russia and America preferred to continue nuclear tests underground once they had achieved all they needed through atmospheric nuclear tests.

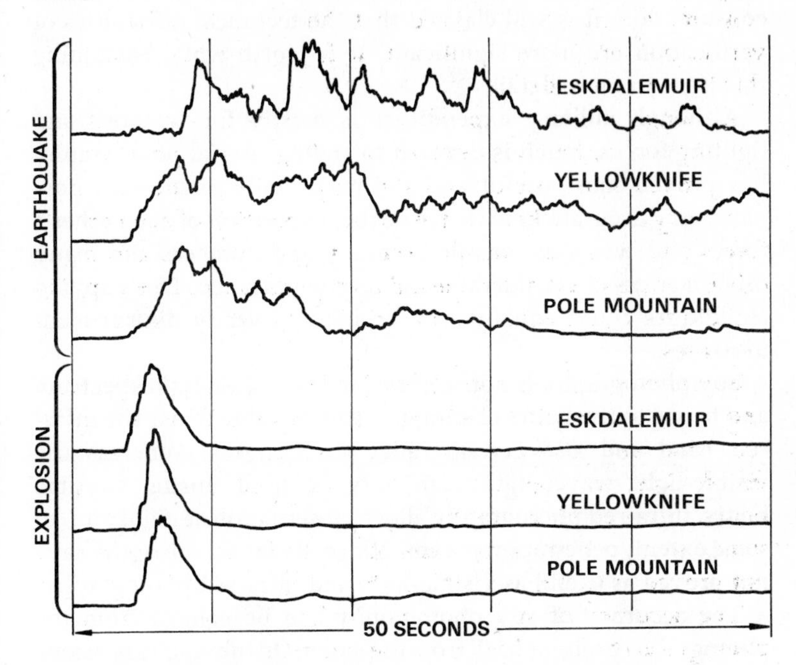

Seismic records of underground nuclear explosions are readily distinguished from earthquakes by their shorter duration. The three upper traces were produced by a Libyan earthquake, the bottom three by a French nuclear test in Algeria

The PTBT is indeed a great advance, for it has cut dramatically the major radioactive pollution of the atmosphere. But it has not halted or even slowed down the nuclear arms race. And whilst the signatories to the PTBT continue to test underground, France and China repeat what America, Britain and Russia were doing at the equivalent stage in their nuclear developments.

Satellite observation

So the main stumbling block in the way of disarmament is simply a lack of willingness to disarm. Nevertheless, for public consumption, it is still claimed that the technical difficulties of verification are more significant. It is worth-while examining this issue in more detail.

Although military expenditure is mostly for weapons and fighting forces, much is devoted to spying. Aerial photography has proved most useful and the major military powers now have very accurate knowledge of the disposition of each other's forces and weapons, missile accuracy and numbers and many other matters of considerable military importance. These spying techniques could equally well be used to verify disarmament measures.

Spy photography is not confined to the visible-light spectrum and hence to the hours of sunlight. It is possible to use the infra-red band and also certain radar wavelengths. Whereas the visible-light wavelengths can only be used during daytime hours, infra-red photography allows observation at night and, to some extent, penetration of camouflage. Radar wavelengths have not proved as useful as visible-light and infra-red photography.

The accuracy of spy photography can be gauged from the photographs brought back from the moon. On the Apollo missions a typical camera had a focal length of two feet and, from an altitude of approximately sixty miles above the lunar surface, obtained three-foot ground resolutions (that is, it picked up objects as small as about three feet). Cameras for satellite photography have a focal length of more than eight feet and so, from an altitude of say 100 miles, the ground resolution would be just over a foot. The clarity of the pictures from photo reconnaissance satellites is now limited more by atmospheric effects than anything else.

Artificial satellites are better than aircraft for photographic reconnaissance because they have no engines and so do not vibrate. This means that the clarity of photographs from artificial

An aerial photograph of central London. Many important features could be picked out with careful study

Francis Gary Powers, pilot of an American U-2 spy-plane, was shot down over Soviet territory in 1960

satellites can be as good as from aircraft, despite the greater height from which they are taken. They are also preferable because, apart from the technical advantages, aircraft are vulnerable to anti-aircraft fire from below – as U S pilot Gary Powers found out in 1961 when his U-2 flight was abruptly terminated.

In general it is easier to find an object on a photograph than to decide what it is. All the same an extended object such as a railway can be distinguished even when its width is less than the minimum ground resolution: it is even possible to pick out telegraph wires. In practice, analysis is limited primarily by the huge amount of data collected.

If all the Soviet Union were constantly photographed in minute detail, every existing U S computer would be involved on this task alone. To overcome this difficulty, *two* sets of photographs are taken: the first to identify interesting targets (*surveillance*) and the second to rephotograph the more interesting areas in greater detail (*close-look*).

Early surveillance satellites stayed aloft for three to four weeks and carried a wide-angle, low-resolution camera. When near to an appropriate ground station, the exposed film (already developed aboard the space craft) was scanned by on-board electronic devices and the resulting signals were transmitted to earth by radio. This provided the information needed for a subsequent close-look expedition. As high resolution (that is, detailed accuracy) was not needed for surveillance, the photographs were rarely recovered.

The earliest US reconnaissance satellite (SAMOS) was first used in 1960, shortly after Gary Powers's flight over the USSR. SAMOS was placed in a polar orbit varying in altitude from 300 to 350 miles. Later satellites had an orbital life of three to four weeks with a perigree (lowest orbital point) about 100 miles above the earth's surface. Since 1966 these have provided constant and virtually full coverage of the USSR and complete coverage of China.

Close-look cameras have a very high resolution and a relatively narrow field of view. Early close-look satellites were larger than those used for surveillance and remained in near-polar orbit for about five days before film recovery – which was usually accomplished by the ejection of a capsule containing the film and its collection from the sea. (More often nowadays the capsule is recovered in mid-air. When the capsule falls to about ten miles from earth, a parachute opens and is caught by a trapeze-like cable attached to a transport aircraft.)

The Discovery recoverable-capsule satellites are heavier than surveillance satellites and have a lower orbit (perigree typically eighty miles) to take detailed (close-look) photographs. From about 1971 onwards a new generation of observation satellites was introduced, known unofficially as the Big Bird. It is launched by the powerful Titan 3D booster rocket, weighs about 10 tons and combines area surveillance with close-look, the latter taking place on the orbit immediately after the surveillance orbit over the same spot.

A Soviet espionage programme similar to that of the US appears to be taking place with their Cosmos satellite launches. This programme incorporates a long and consistent series of eight-day and thirteen-day flights, presumably for reconnaissance. They probably look at the same things as the Americans but they use different techniques. For example, there are no Soviet satellites in high orbits as are used as part of the US Vela nuclear detection system (to record fallout radioactivity and explosion

X-rays). Nor does the Cosmos programme include satellites with orbits that might be expected to provide early warning of a nuclear attack.

The 'amateur' analysis of Cosmos satellite launches carried out by the Kettering Grammar School (Northants) tracking group suggests that there may be several different types of flight within the eight-day and thirteen-day groups. The thirteen-day satellites sometimes make small manoeuvres, about half are recoverable and, for more than a decade, at least one such satellite has been in orbit for two thirds of the time. Although details of the Soviet programme are still a matter of conjecture, there can be little doubt that this scrutiny of the USA and her NATO allies is as thorough as the American and NATO scrutiny of the Soviet Union.

Certainly since 1962, and probably earlier, the United States has had detailed information on the number and location of Soviet strategic missiles. In 1967 President Johnson claimed that satellite reconnaissance was worth 'ten times' as much as the US space programme because 'I know how many missiles the enemy has'. Intelligence analysts are continuously watching silo construction and transport to and from launch sites and, although photography does not penetrate buildings, infra-red and multi-spectral techniques also indicate what goes on inside – particularly when new activities involve changes in standard operating procedures. Multi-spectral analysis is achieved by taking photographs of the same area through different colour filters, thus obtaining highly accurate prints of the colour spectrum of the objects photographed – rather like a three-dimensional view from above.

It has proved impossible to hide large objects by camouflage. If the surrounding ground has temperatures or emission characteristics which differ from the nearby terrain, this will show on an infra-red picture. Moreover the installation of camouflaged objects takes time and can be observed by satellites. Few, if any, items of major military significance are small: missile sites and similar military installations cannot escape detection. In the same way the development and testing of new weapons involves activities which can be observed by spy satellites – which is why we can compare strategic nuclear forces (as in Chapter 6).

The photographs help to identify missile systems, to detect changes in operating procedures and to monitor testing programmes. The satellites are used to watch industrial facilities, including shipyards, for the construction of submarines and plants and for the assembly of missiles. Virtually all the problems of verification of arms control and disarmament agreements have therefore been *solved* by technical advances in satellite photography and analysis.

A radio microphone camouflaged as a shirt button can pick up sound 50 feet away

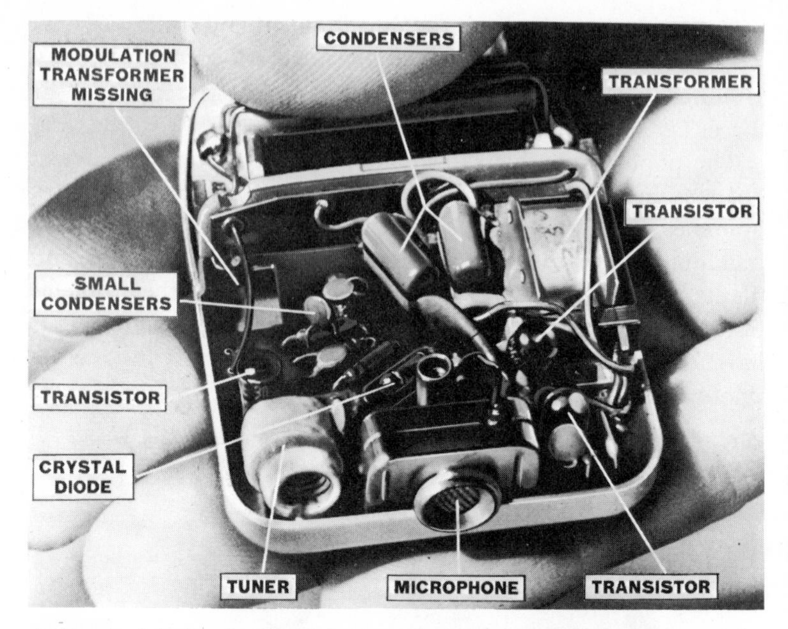

A 'bugging' device that fits into the palm of the hand. It has a range of 250 yards and operates for 30 hours

Other types of observation

Even the *performance* of military equipment can be deduced. Since as early as 1955 US radar in Samson, Turkey, has tracked missile tests from the Soviet launch site at Kasutin Yar, north-west of the Caspian Sea. Several fixed land-based radars are also available: they watch where Soviet re-entry vehicles fall. From their trajectory it is possible to decide if the missiles have one or more warheads and whether these are guided to targets (MIRVs) or are simply fragments scattering on burn up.

Over-the-horizon (OTH) radar is used to monitor missile tests. Stations at Okinawa (an island south of Japan), Cyprus and Orford Ness (now abandoned) can detect disturbances in the ionosphere caused by the gas exhaust of a rocket. Since each type of missile disturbs the ionosphere somewhat differently, it can be identified by its characteristic OTH signature. All Soviet long-range missiles can be discovered this way.

Apart from photography, other verification techniques are available. Electronic eavesdropping is one of the most useful, since conversations over radio and telephone links are easily 'tapped'. Indoor conversations can be bugged. Electronic eavesdropping satellites can listen in to short-range radio transmissions. As no government can arrange all its business outdoors, it follows that the *intentions* of the military are often known even before construction of new weapons begins.

All these observational techniques were developed for military reasons and were originally intended to provide early warning of new military developments or even of an attack. But they also provide the means by which arms control and disarmament agreements can be monitored.

9. Disarmament

Over the years they have worked their way over the whole canvas of the subject and could now well produce watertight treaties at the drop of a hat, if only the political decisions were taken.

The Times,
on the 508th meeting of the
UN Disarmament Committee

Satellite observation and other unilateral inspection methods have proved more than adequate for arms control treaties such as SALT-1. The same techniques have even greater potential for disarmament since whilst it might be possible for a country to disguise the type of weapons it holds, it would be extremely difficult to disguise the fact that it holds weapons of some sort.

For example, an agreement to limit MIRVed missiles but not all missiles might be difficult to monitor without on-site inspection and suspicions would continue. But an agreement to disarm by destroying *all* missiles could be checked by satellite photography and there would be little opportunity for cheating.

But cheating, or the fear of cheating, is not the only obstacle to disarmament. Whilst arms were being destroyed, it might be feared that one side had a *temporary* military lead and would be tempted to exploit this advantage. For example, if one side originally had more missiles than the other, then the destruction of missiles would be of greater help to the side previously having fewer missiles. So the process of disarmament has to maintain *relative* military strengths as it proceeds. Otherwise, if a political dispute arose during this period, war, or at least rearmament, could be started once more.

Although General and Complete Disarmament (GCD) would leave all sides equal – with nothing – the road to GCD is complicated by this need to maintain at least a rough balance for all parties. This is why the plans for GCD almost agreed by America and Russia in the early 1960s all envisaged a short period (five to ten years) to dismantle the entire war machines of the superpowers.

One proposal put forward from the Pugwash Movement appears to overcome most difficulties. It would be for each country *itself* to divide its territory into areas which are to be completely disarmed. Then it would be for the other side to decide the *order* in which the areas disarm. (This would be rather like sharing an orange between two squabbling children: one child divides the orange and the other chooses. This procedure makes sure that the divider takes good care that the orange is exactly equally divided.)

Each country would divide its own territory into, say, twenty geographical areas which it considers of equal military significance. The other side then would choose which one of these twenty areas should be completely disarmed. If this process took about six months, at the end of that period all parties would have reduced their armaments by 5 per cent and thus would be in the same relative position with respect to each other. Then, by choosing the second areas for disarmament, in the following six months a further 5 per cent of the armaments would be eliminated and again all would remain at the same relative strength. This technique could make General and Complete Disarmament a manageable process and gradually extend the areas over the world in which there would be total disarmament.

Although this proposal has not been adopted (or discussed), arms control by systematically extending nuclear-free zones is a realistic prospect. At one time the British and American governments were in favour of first Central Europe, and later the rest of Europe, becoming nuclear-free. (Unfortunately there is now more talk of the EEC becoming a nuclear power comparable with the superpowers and little or no talk about these earlier ideas.)

In other parts of the world there are nuclear-free zones already: in Latin America and Antarctica, with good prospects for Africa and parts of Asia. This may help disarmament, since negotiations between the superpowers would be simplified if all other powers were non-nuclear.

The Comprehensive Test Ban Treaty (CTBT)

In the words of Kurt Waldheim, Secretary General of the United Nations, agreement to ban all nuclear-weapons tests would be the most important single measure to halt the nuclear arms race. Since it is very simple to detect nuclear tests, whether above or below ground level, it is also extremely easy to verify that they have been stopped.

Although the USA and USSR are gradually moving towards agreement on a CTBT, progress is sufficiently slow to allow military planners to continue with all the nuclear tests they 'need'. So France and China, and the 'near-nuclear' countries, are able to claim that the superpowers intend to keep their lead and are making no concessions to the rest of the world.

There is one rider necessary to the assertion that a CTBT will be easy to monitor. There have been suggestions that 'peaceful nuclear explosions' (PNEs) should be excluded from a CTBT on the grounds that nuclear explosions might be useful for earth-moving, oil recovery, etc. Since there is no certain way of distinguishing between a peaceful and a warlike explosion, this would make the treaty meaningless – another example of the maxim that 'the only reliable ban is a complete ban'!

The Non-Proliferation Treaty (NPT)

This treaty is probably the most serious attempt so far made to halt the nuclear arms race and it has been ratified by more than ninety countries. In effect it is a 'deal' between nuclear and non-nuclear powers in which *non-nuclear powers* agree 'not to receive . . . manufacture or otherwise acquire nuclear weapons or other nuclear explosive devices . . .' (Article II) provided that *the nuclear powers* 'pursue negotiations in good faith on effective measures relating to cessation of the nuclear arms race at an early date and to nuclear disarmament and on a treaty on general and complete disarmament, under strict and effective international control' (Article VI).

As with so many other partial measures, the NPT was signed for a variety of reasons and so is built on fragile foundations. The nuclear powers appreciate the danger of nuclear proliferation

Soviet Foreign Minister Andrei Gromyko and President Nixon sign an interim agreement on the limitation of anti-ballistic missile sites in the USA and USSR. Left to right: *Soviet Ambassador Anatoly Dobrynin; Gromyko; Nixon; US Secretary of State, William Rogers (1972)*

but they are not as concerned about their own nuclear weapons. The non-nuclear powers fear a world-wide nuclear war and see the commitment to nuclear disarmament in Article VI as a major feature of the treaty.

Countries such as India, South Africa, Israel and Brazil did not sign the NPT on the grounds that it contained no guarantee of nuclear disarmament and so seemed more like a device to prevent near-nuclear countries like themselves from acquiring nuclear status. Another weakness of the treaty is that it does not stop the transfer of nuclear-power technology to non-nuclear countries. But such a transfer enables a non-nuclear country to make plutonium, and thus to construct an atomic bomb. In exactly this way India (a non-signatory) developed her first nuclear explosive device by using plutonium manufactured in a nuclear-power plant supplied to her by Canada (a signatory of the NPT).

Whether or not the NPT succeeds depends above all else upon the progress made by the nuclear powers to nuclear disarmament. If good progress is made, the non-nuclear countries will not have the same urge to join the nuclear arms race. The Strategic Arms Limitation Talks (SALT) have been presented as the response of the nuclear powers to this commitment under Article VI of the NPT.

If these negotiations lead to nuclear disarmament, there will be good prospects that no more countries will 'go nuclear'. Unfortunately, at the time of writing, the so-called spirit of détente has not even curbed the nuclear arms race. As shown in Chapter 6, the limitations on missile numbers following SALT-1 have prevented neither increased numbers of nuclear warheads nor improvements in accuracy to make the warheads much more lethal. Moreover there are disturbing signs that ways are being found to circumvent even the meagre limitations of the 1972 SALT-1 agreement.

The Long-Range Cruise Missile (LRCM)

Chief amongst these is a Long-Range Cruise Missile (LRCM) which can be launched from a variety of vehicles (submarines, ships and even a passenger-carrying 747 jet). The LRCM will carry its own guidance mechanism (which could be linked to a Satellite Global Positioning system), driven by an on-board mini-computer, and will be able to change and correct its course during flight. As this modern-day 'buzz-bomb' is not a free-fall

Long-range cruise missiles will find their way to the target by comparing their 'memory' of a digital map of the terrain against observations whilst cruising

0	0	0	0	0	0	0	0	0	0	0	0	0	0	0	0	0	0	0	0	0	0	9	14	17	17	18	18	18	18
0	0	0	0	0	0	0	0	0	0	0	0	0	0	0	0	0	0	0	0	0	1	10	16	18	18	18	18	18	18
0	0	0	0	0	0	0	1	0	0	0	0	0	0	0	0	0	0	0	0	0	9	15	18	18	18	18	18	18	18
0	0	0	0	0	0	0	1	0	0	0	0	0	0	0	0	0	0	0	0	0	15	19	18	18	18	18	18	18	18
0	0	0	0	0	0	0	1	0	0	0	0	0	0	0	0	0	0	0	0	8	18	20	18	18	18	18	18	18	18
0	0	0	1	0	0	1	1	0	0	0	0	0	0	0	0	0	0	0	0	10	18	21	18	18	18	18	18	18	18
0	0	0	1	0	0	3	3	2	1	0	0	0	0	0	0	0	0	0	0	13	18	18	17	17	18	18	18	18	18
0	0	0	1	1	2	4	4	3	2	0	0	0	0	0	0	0	0	0	1	14	18	18	16	16	17	18	18	18	18
0	0	0	1	2	2	4	4	3	3	0	0	0	0	0	0	0	0	0	9	15	18	18	17	17	17	16	17	18	18
0	0	1	1	1	2	4	5	3	3	1	0	0	0	0	0	0	0	0	10	14	16	16	15	15	17	18	18	18	18
0	0	0	0	1	2	4	4	4	4	3	0	0	0	0	0	0	0	6	10	12	15	15	14	14	16	15	18	18	18
0	0	0	0	1	4	6	5	5	5	6	2	0	0	0	0	0	0	4	10	9	12	13	12	12	14	16	17	18	18
0	0	0	0	0	7	8	6	5	6	8	7	2	0	0	0	0	0	4	6	7	10	11	9	12	14	16	17	18	18
0	0	0	0	0	3	7	7	6	9	14	9	5	0	0	0	0	0	0	2	6	8	10	11	12	13	15	17	18	18
0	0	0	0	0	2	4	7	8	14	16	16	10	7	0	0	0	0	0	1	4	6	10	11	11	12	15	17	17	18
0	0	0	0	0	1	4	8	10	16	20	18	12	10	6	0	0	0	0	0	2	2	5	9	11	12	13	14	16	16
0	0	0	0	0	0	4	6	10	16	20	18	12	12	9	7	0	0	0	1	2	3	4	8	9	11	12	13	14	15
0	0	0	0	0	1	4	8	10	12	13	19	17	12	11	8	1	0	0	0	2	3	3	7	8	10	12	12	12	13
0	0	0	0	0	1	5	9	10	8	6	8	10	12	10	5	2	0	0	0	2	3	4	5	6	7	9	10	12	13
0	0	0	0	0	1	7	11	7	6	6	8	8	9	7	3	1	0	0	1	3	5	7	6	7	6	7	8	11	12
0	0	0	0	0	1	7	12	14	14	6	6	7	8	1	1	1	0	0	1	5	7	10	8	8	8	7	6	7	10
0	0	0	0	0	1	7	12	14	13	6	7	7	7	5	1	1	1	0	1	7	9	10	10	10	10	10	9	6	7
0	0	0	0	0	2	7	12	13	6	6	7	8	7	6	1	1	1	0	1	2	7	10	11	12	13	14	12	12	10
0	0	0	0	0	2	7	12	8	6	6	7	7	7	7	1	1	1	1	2	2	3	4	10	11	13	16	16	14	12
0	0	0	0	0	2	7	11	7	7	6	6	6	6	7	4	4	4	3	2	3	4	4	5	7	10	13	16	16	14
0	0	0	0	0	1	6	10	8	7	6	6	6	7	8	5	5	5	4	3	5	8	8	7	5	9	13	16	16	15
0	0	0	0	1	1	6	10	9	8	6	6	6	7	8	6	6	4	4	4	7	10	10	7	6	8	12	13	14	15
0	0	0	5	4	6	7	10	9	8	9	6	6	6	7	7	8	4	4	4	5	9	10	12	6	7	10	12	14	15
0	0	5	6	6	9	8	10	11	10	9	8	6	6	6	7	8	8	6	4	6	9	10	8	6	7	7	10	14	15
0	0	5	8	9	11	13	15	12	10	9	9	8	6	6	7	7	8	8	8	8	8	10	7	6	6	6	10	13	14
0	0	6	6	9	11	17	16	14	10	8	8	8	8	6	6	6	8	9	10	11	11	11	11	7	6	6	7	10	11

ballistic missile, the US government has argued that it is not covered by the SALT-1 limitations.

The LRCM has great accuracy (CEP = approximately 100 feet) which gives it a very high lethality at a relatively low cost. At 1975 prices the 'cost per unit kill probability' of the Minuteman III ICBM was around $700,000. By comparison the LRCM unit lethality will cost no more than $3,000. British interest needs no further explanation!

Another serious aspect of LRCMs is that, unlike all the ICBMs, SLBMs and the other strategic-weapons delivery systems described earlier, they have some immunity from satellite inspection. The high accuracy of the LRCMs depends upon the light, miniature and relatively inexpensive electronic devices which are mounted on a missile that is typically under one yard in diameter and less than six yards long. These missiles can be loaded with nuclear *or* conventional explosives. It will be extremely difficult for satellite observations to monitor how

Cruise missiles

many possess nuclear warheads and impossible to assess how many are programmed for intercontinental targets.

LRCMs will make nuclear proliferation far easier than hitherto. Because they can be used to carry conventional explosives, they may be sold to any country that shows a commercial interest. Countries that could not consider ICBMs and SLBMs because of their cost, and hence have not acquired nuclear weapons, might change their attitude if LRCMs became available.

The LRCM is a good example of the way in which technological advances can outstrip political and military needs. Partial Arms Control agreements such as SALT-1 do no more than impair the advances in new weaponry whilst the momentum of these developments renders the previous arms control measures worthless. The limitations on ICBMs and SLBMs will contribute no more to peace in 1980 than would the banning of bows and arrows in 1939. A *total* halt in all arms developments is an essential prerequisite for any disarmament. Without this there can be no guarantee that any partial measures, however well considered, will not be superseded by ever more dangerous new weapons.

Would disarmament measures be circumvented?

The way that countries have circumvented arms control measures leads many people to believe that this would happen also with disarmament. In addition, even if complete disarmament were to be achieved, there seems nothing to prevent countries rearming once more should they so desire. If these views are correct, genuine disarmament must be a hopeless dream.

There are three good reasons for discounting these fears, two of which have been mentioned already. In the first place, disarmament is much easier to control than is arms limitation in the midst of a continuing arms race. All methods of delivering nuclear weapons, such as LRCMs, would be automatically prohibited in the context of disarmament and so would their use for

The cartoon on this page and those on pp. 169, 177 and 191 are taken from Nursery Rhymes for a Nuclear Age *by Chris Plant and Jim Hayes, published by the ATOM Committee (Against Testing On Mururoa atoll), Suva, Fiji*

conventional explosives. So new technological advances are unlikely to supersede the terms of a disarmament measure as has so often occurred with arms control.

Secondly, the process of disarmament is far more likely to lead to an increase in mutual trust and understanding and a lowering of tension than is arms control. Whereas disarmament strikes at one of the main causes of the arms race – mutual fear –

arms control can actually increase suspicion since the balance of terror is maintained exactly as before and every action is scrutinized to detect potential new developments.

The third reason is more complex. As is well known, many powerful industrial and commercial interests rely upon the arms race for their prosperity and have good reason to fear disarmament. They put pressure on governments and make disarmament more difficult. In 1961 President Eisenhower warned:

> We have been compelled to create a permanent armaments industry of vast proportions ... We must not fail to comprehend its grave implications ... In the councils of governments we must guard against the acquisition of unwarranted influence, whether sought or unsought, by the military–industrial complex.

Once disarmament got underway the power of the military–industrial complex would be reduced. This would be so whether the industries switched to peaceful production or suffered a

US President Eisenhower with British Prime Minister Macmillan (1959)

decline at the expense of other industry. In either event there would be more people with a vested interest in maintaining the momentum of disarmament and less with an interest in additional production of armaments. Thus, provided disarmament proceeded at a reasonable pace, once under way there would be less and less internal opposition to the policy.

In summary, disarmament is not only more desirable than arms control, it may be easier to implement also. Once effected it would be hard to return to the conditions of the arms race because the major reasons for that race, both external (mutual fear) and internal (vested interests), will have been removed.

10. War as a way of life

War is horrible. There is no question about it. But so is peace. And it is proper . . . to compare the horror of war and the horror of peace and see how much worse it is.

Herman Kahn

War in our time has become an anachronism. Whatever the case in the past, wars in the future can serve no useful purpose.

Dwight Eisenhower

Mankind is accustomed to war. For thousands of years there have been wars between tribes, kingdoms and nations. Historians can show that much of this bloodshed has actually benefited human progress. Warlike behaviour is now thoroughly ingrained in our make-up with the result that many people believe disarmament is not practicable.

There is moreover some evidence that human beings have an innate aggressive instinct which may have been necessary for survival in the past. So the argument that 'You can't change human nature' is used as an explanation and excuse for past wars and for the continuing arms race. It is often claimed that the popularity of war games and war stories indicates that warfare satisfies a basic biological need.

Yet war has not *always* been a feature of human society:

at one time it was unknown. It became significant at a particular stage in history and, by the same token, could disappear in the future. An understanding of the history and evolution of warfare is beyond the scope of this book, but the following brief review may help explain how war may be eradicated.

What is 'war'?

War is not simply a large-scale domestic squabble. It is an *organized* activity requiring active and continual *preparation*. For this reason it must not be confused with the spontaneous arguments and occasional fisticuffs that often enliven family life. Domestic disputes took place, no doubt, in early primitive

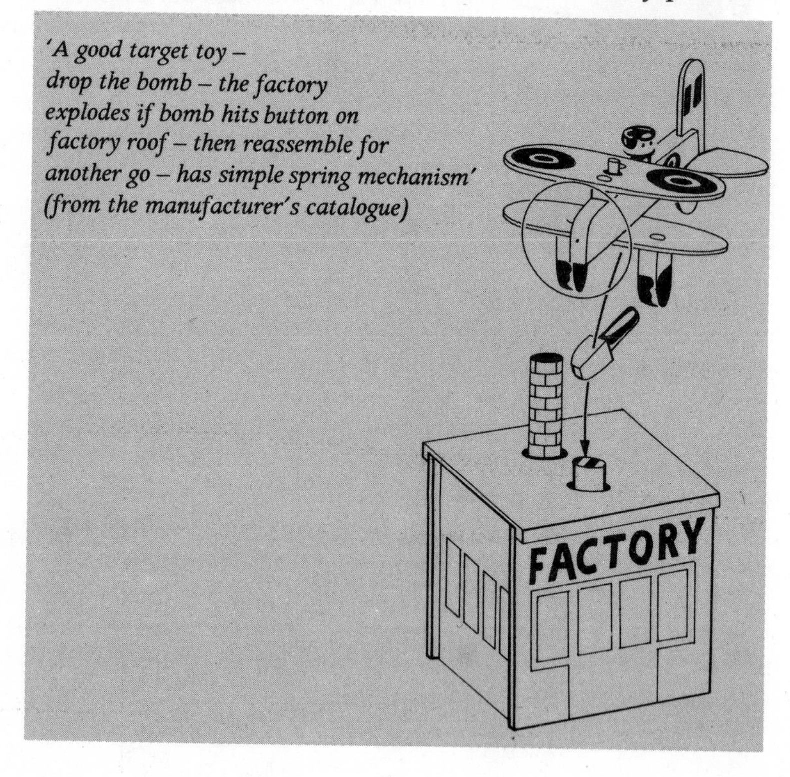

'A good target toy – drop the bomb – the factory explodes if bomb hits button on factory roof – then reassemble for another go – has simple spring mechanism' (from the manufacturer's catalogue)

communities but there were neither special weapons available for killing people nor trained professional fighters. The weapons of early communities were used for hunting and farming, not against fellow human beings (except presumably in the heat of the moment).

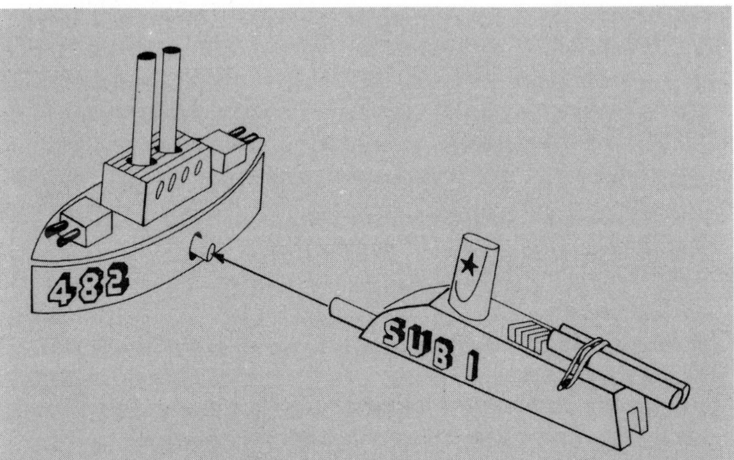

One of the best toys I have seen for little ones this year is the Ship and Submarine. A wooden destroyer, of sorts, is rapidly assembled from a collection of pieces and a spring-loaded core is laid in the heart of the ship. From the ship's side protrudes a small end of a dowel. You then take the submarine and push in its longer dowel of a torpedo until it engages with a click. Hold the sub firmly, aiming the torpedo at the destroyer and press the firing lever. The entire destroyer blows up, all the pieces flying about and falling on the floor, but not close enough to the submarine's 'captain' so as to hurt him. Then you start rebuilding the ship for more destruction.

Solid and likely to last for ages, and to give pleasure for that long.

(from *The Times*, 9 November 1973)

The idea of war

Margaret Mead

Warfare, by which I mean recognized conflict between two groups *as groups*, in which each group puts an army (even if the army is only fifteen pygmies) into the field to fight and kill . . . is an invention like any other of the inventions in terms of which we order our lives, such as writing, marriage, cooking our food instead of eating it raw, trial by jury or burial of the dead, and so on . . .

There are peoples even today who have no warfare. Of these the Eskimo are perhaps the most conspicuous examples, but the Lepchas of Sikkim . . . are as good. Neither of these peoples understands war, not even defensive warfare. The idea of warfare is lacking and this idea is as essential to really carrying on war as an alphabet . . . is to writing. But whereas the Lepchas are a gentle, unquarrelsome people . . . the Eskimo are not a mild and meek people; many of them are turbulent and troublesome . . . Here are men faced with hunger, men faced with loss of their wives, men faced with the threat of extermination by other men, and here are orphan children, growing up miserably with no one to care for them, mocked and neglected by those about them. The personality necessary for war, the circumstances necessary to goad men to desperation are present, but there is no war . . .

[In contrast are] the pygmy peoples of the Andaman Islands in the Bay of Bengal. The Andamans also represent an exceedingly low level of society; they are a hunting and food-gathering people; they live in tiny hordes without any class stratification; their houses are simpler than the snow houses of the Eskimo. But they knew about warfare. The army might contain only fifteen determined pygmies marching in a straight line, but it was the real thing none the less. Tiny army met tiny army in open battle, blows were exchanged, casualties suffered, and the state of warfare could only be concluded by a peacemaking ceremony . . .

So simple peoples and civilized peoples, mild peoples and violent, assertive peoples, will all go to war if they have the invention, just as those peoples who have the custom of duelling will have duels and peoples who have the pattern of vendetta will indulge in vendetta. And, conversely, peoples who do not know of duelling will not fight duels, even though their wives are seduced and their daughters ravished; they may on occasion commit murder but they will not fight duels.

(from *Warfare Is Only an Invention – Not A Biological Necessity*, 1940)

There were good reasons for this. Early communities lived at subsistence level and there was neither wealth nor better living standards to be obtained from murder. On the contrary the widely dispersed population of early societies needed many hands for the collective work of hunting and food gathering so that all might prosper. Inter-community fighting would have been suicidal, because numbers were essential for survival as a community. Just as farming is a relatively recent human activity (about ten thousand years) so is war (about five thousand years) – and even today some communities exist without knowing armed conflict.

But, granted that warfare is an invention, why was it adopted by, for example, the North American Indians, and not by their near-neighbours the Eskimos? One might have expected martial behaviour to become dominant in all communities, but this has not happened in every case. Societies do not automatically adopt warfare once it has been invented: other conditions also have to be satisfied. War has first to be worthwhile for the community, *as a community* – a condition never satisfied for the Eskimo peoples who live in widely dispersed settlements and have little scope for territorial disputes. The degree of sophistication of a society and its technology has little relevance since primitive communities, given the conditions of economic conflict, do make war.

Communal warfare

War has been a consequence of man's success as a species. As mankind became more populous, tribes began to fight over each other's territory. Thus began economic conflict between human beings – the first essential prerequisite for war.

However, the character of this early fighting was very different from what followed. An entire community fought to defend or occupy a pasture or hunting ground, but the outcome of the battle did not alter the way of life of the victor or the vanquished – all remained hunters or farmers. Indeed it often happened that the surviving members of the defeated tribe became full members of the victorious tribe. This early fighting may be termed *communal warfare* and has more in common with civil wars or guerrilla wars than most major wars of history.

As economies developed beyond subsistence level, communities grew larger and more sophisticated. People began to specialize in certain tasks: for instance, some became toolmakers, some craftsmen and others remained unskilled workers. As a result disagreements began to arise about how the society's wealth should be shared. Some people claimed to deserve more than others because of their special skills. Eventually the old communal societies collapsed.

The new social structures that then arose were divided into a hierarchy of specialists; depending upon status and property ownership, people belonged to particular classes. Egyptian, Greek and Roman societies were extreme examples of 'class-divided societies' with ten or twenty times as many slaves as freemen.

Professional warfare

For our purpose, the important point is that a divided society needs power to regulate and maintain these divisions. The task of coercion was entrusted to the warrior whose job was to keep 'law and order' for the slave owners (often the warriors were themselves slave owners) and to obtain a ready supply of new slaves. In short, warriors fought on behalf of the community (or, more accurately perhaps, on behalf of the rulers of the community).

This is the second feature of most modern warfare: it involves societies with *professional* fighters. These police the community internally and defend the community against external foes, and are maintained by the rest of the community through taxes of various kinds.

As antagonisms within a community grew, and were formalized and contained by laws and traditions, so antagonisms between communities also developed. Eventually 'empires' were established, in which widely separated communities were controlled by allegiance to a dominant tribe (for example, the Tartars under Genghis Khan) or a city (for example, Rome or Alexandria). The central authority then exacted tribute in the form of slaves, goods and taxes and so became even more powerful. At its zenith the Roman Empire controlled most of present-day Europe as well as parts of Africa and Asia Minor.

Antagonisms between empires made their boundaries a constant battleground and it became necessary to make continual preparations for warfare. From this time onwards, war has been a *permanent* feature of developed society. As a result, war between communities became a major preoccupation of the rulers, and many rulers were chosen for their fighting ability.

From being an occasional collective activity on the part of the entire community, war became a continuous specialized activity on behalf of the rulers.

It would be wrong to suggest, however, that such wars only benefited rulers. The Roman Empire brought order and a more developed society to its colonies and probably raised living standards in the process. Trade routes were made secure by warfare: over 1,000 years after the fall of the Roman Empire the exchange of English wool for Indian spices benefited communities along the entire length of the trade route. But generally, as trade and shipping developed and new countries were discovered, trading relationships changed in character. They became unequal and the cause of continual friction. Spanish and Portuguese adventurers stripped the largely pacific civilizations of the Americas of gold and silver and the English plundered their homeward-bound ships. The Anglo–Spanish wars of the sixteenth century resulted from this rivalry for plunder. This kind of war was simply state-aided piracy.

It is clear then that, until the nationalist wars of the nineteenth century, war was primarily a contest between monarchies for territory or money, and the aristocratic élite were the only people with an interest in victory. Most people had to be persuaded to fight to support wars: they were therefore often fought for ostensibly idealistic reasons – religious wars are a good example. The Crusades aimed to secure access to the Holy City for pilgrims, but in addition they helped to secure trade routes to India and the East.

Nationalist wars

Nowadays nearly everyone is concerned to avoid the tragedies that war brings. This change was well under way long before the advent of modern weapons. People cared about the outcome of the Napoleonic wars: the whole French nation was mobilized, not just the ruling élite. The genius of Napoleon was not only military but political: he was able to enthuse masses to rally

An M.P. called Frank in Tahiti
Said he felt that he just wasn't free:
"If the French want to test,
Then surely it's best
If they blow up their bombs in Paree?"

Mayor Francis Sanford, French Polynesia's Representative to the French National Assembly, was reported in the Fiji Times *(November 1972) as saying: 'They tell us the tests are clean. If it is true, why don't they let off the explosions in France?' The same paper had earlier (September 1971) reported the French Ambassador to Fiji, Count Christian de Nicolay, as claiming that the risk was lessened by having the tests in the Pacific: 'Below you in France you have 50 million people; here there is nothing.'*

behind the national flag. Chauvinistic propaganda had become an essential instrument of warfare.

The failure of the Americans in Vietnam illustrates how difficult it is to win a war today without the complete support of the people. Although the US forces suffered many military setbacks they were at all times vastly stronger than the Vietnamese: even now they have the military strength to annihilate Vietnam. The American government failed because they lost the political will to continue the fight – in other words they were unable to convince enough Americans that they were in the right. By contrast the people they were fighting were convinced of the rightness of their cause and, despite their far greater losses, continued their struggle.

Although the chivalrous professionals-only war has long disappeared, the concept lingers on. As late as 1920 the President of the International Committee of the Red Cross wrote:

> The Committee considers it very desirable that war should resume its former character, that is to say, that it should be a struggle between armies and not between populations. The civilian population must, as far as possible, remain outside the struggle and its consequences.

The 'civilized warfare' embodied in the 'rules' of the St Petersburg, Hague and Geneva Conventions owes much to this philosophy. Although medieval knights might act cruelly against rebellions from their own serfs, they would not use the medieval equivalent of APW against non-combatants. Warfare was strictly a matter for the leaders of society. Fortunately people are no longer prepared to remain 'outside the struggle' and this offers hope that wars may eventually be abolished altogether.

World wars

The eighteenth and nineteenth centuries saw vast industrial, social and economic changes in the richer countries, especially Britain. Many more goods were produced than the people could buy (or needed). Whereas the early empires guaranteed *supplies* of raw materials (wool, slaves etc.), empires now also could guarantee *markets* for manufactured goods. The expansion of empires in the nineteenth century resulted from the economic pressure to gain such markets.

By the turn of the century unequal trading relationships were commonplace with the whole world divided among the rich countries. (In 1876 11 per cent of Africa belonged to European powers; by 1900 it was 90 per cent.) Further expansion then had to be at the expense of other industrial countries.

The British Empire enabled British manufactured goods to be exported, under protection, to India, Canada and other countries as well as securing raw materials. Germany, the last major European country to industrialize, was denied access to these

The conquest of Africa, 1880

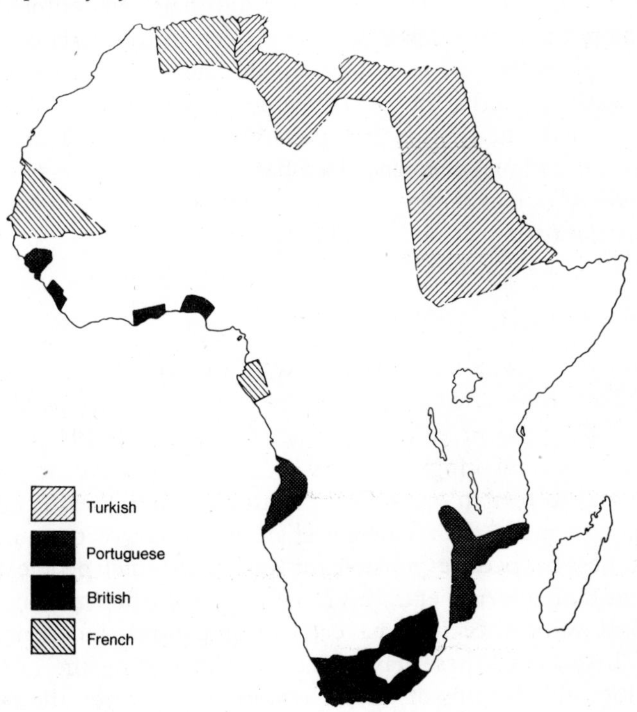

markets and suffered accordingly. The First World War thus involved competition over *exports* (as opposed to raw materials) and affected virtually every country. It resulted in the re-division of Germany's colonies amongst the victors.

In the Second World War Japan and Germany again tried unsuccessfully to re-divide the world in their favour. However, this time the war did help the Germans and the Japanese, albeit indirectly. Colonial independence movements were strengthened and the empires of Britain, France and Holland soon disintegrated. This means that German and Japanese industry now can sell to most of the former colonies, markets that were previously denied them. (Germany and Japan also had the incidental advantage that, after the war, they were not allowed to waste too much on arms: this enabled them to invest more money in industrial plant and machinery than did their competitors.)

Competition between British and German industrialists continues today but without bloodshed. The main reason is that the really powerful industrialists are *multinational* nowadays and no longer desire the old type of wars. When the British part of a multinational company does badly, investment is switched elsewhere, for example to Germany. So war between the rich industrial nations is now less likely.

Minor wars

These trends do not mean that all wars are over; on the contrary they have intensified other types of conflict and are partly responsible for the *increased* frequency of wars since 1945.

The 'sport of kings' is over because people are no longer prepared to remain 'outside the struggle' when the struggle is simply to make their rulers richer. But this greater political awareness has been responsible for warfare in which people try to change their governments – civil wars, wars of independence, etc.

Most wars since 1945 have been for national independence and, in general, these have succeeded in ending the unequal trading relationships of former empires. Very often the newly independent countries have placed severe restrictions on the activities of foreign investors and used their newly acquired strength to raise prices of raw materials (like oil) substantially. The potential for conflict with former colonial powers thus continues after independence. Wars of independence, and post-independence power struggles (often exacerbated by foreign powers), have greatly increased the incidence of bloodshed in the world since 1945. Moreover many local conflicts now have world-wide implications because they threaten multinational corporations. So these organizations tend to meddle in political affairs to a greater extent than hitherto.

So the economic and political interests of rich industrial nations and multinational corporations are often involved in the minor

The conquest of Africa, 1914

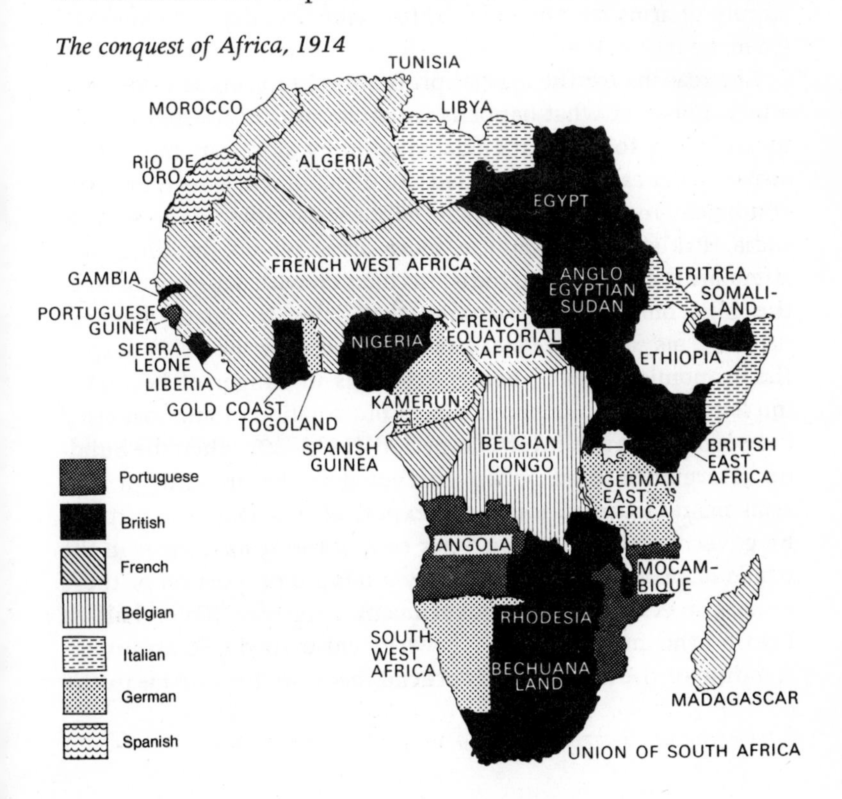

wars. And, although governments and industrialists may no longer wish to see their own people fighting, they are not averse to maintaining it elsewhere. In the Nigerian civil war (1968) French arms were supplied to the Biafran 'rebels' and British and Russian arms to the Nigerian government. In a certain sense the old-style wars continue – but with other people's lives.

The arms trade

The arms race between the superpowers has its own direct influence on the frequency of minor wars. Most of the arms employed are supplied by only a few nations (over 85 per cent from the USA, USSR, UK and France). The motives for the supply of arms may be political (to make friends) or commercial (to make money).

The reasons for the special profitability of arms sales deserve study. Consider what happens when motor cars are sold to, say, India. It may follow that Pakistan will buy more cars but, after a while, fewer cars will be needed and demand will level off in both countries. In contrast, when military equipment is sold to India, Pakistan will require more arms which, in turn, will stimulate further sales to India. In common with drugs, arms have the big commercial advantage that sales stimulate demand. British arms sales have steadily increased over the years despite the economic crises at home. Britain is in danger of becoming 'no longer a nation of shopkeepers but a nation of gun makers'.*

In contrast to the 'inter-war period' (1918–39), when the build-up of armaments was often attributed to the greed of private arms manufacturers, today the export of weapons is controlled by governments. Less than 5 per cent of the arms trade is in the hands of private dealers and only a minute proportion of these dealers operate without government approval. (Over half of British arms manufacture is government-owned.) So an understanding of the arms trade is crucial, because it is one means by

*Mary Kaldor, *The Times*, October 1975.

which the competition between rich countries is extended throughout the world and absorbs local disputes and wars.

An important factor is that, unlike France and Britain, the superpowers generally supply weapons at low prices and low interest rates. But it would be naive to assume that arms manufacturers no longer have any influence on the arms race. The relationship between private arms manufacturers and governments is today as close as it was previously between the warriors and the Roman emperors.

The military–industrial complex

War then is a human activity related to social, economic and political factors. Victory brings economic advantages, sometimes to everybody and usually to rulers and those who influence the rulers of society. This is why President Eisenhower warned against the power and influence of 'the military–industrial complex'. Because arms sales are very profitable, armaments manufacturers are very rich and powerful. They can have a good deal of influence on government policies. If a disarmament proposal looks like succeeding, they can influence public opinion and governments so that the negotiations fail.

Compare the relative indifference of political and military 'experts' when a railway line or coal pit is closed with the furore if 'defence cuts' are suggested. In the former instance we are told that economic progress necessitates that the workers concerned become unemployed. By contrast armaments factories are kept open, allegedly to preserve the workers' livelihoods. An example of this thinking came from Roy Mason, UK Defence Secretary, speaking in Parliament in May 1976: 'If the MRCA contract is cancelled . . . 24,000 jobs would go immediately . . . There would be hardly an aircraft industry left.'

Most armaments factories can be switched to peaceful production. Lucas Aerospace workers have prepared a plan for alternative peaceful employment for their factory which, given the political will, could be quickly implemented. Their advanced electronics knowledge has already come up with a kidney machine, a device to help spina bifida children and retarda braking systems for road transport vehicles. After a particularly bad coach disaster in Yorkshire, in May 1975, the *Sunday Times* commented:

> last week's crash might have been avoided if the coach had been equipped with an extra braking device such as an electro-magnetic retarda which is being fitted to an increasing number of coaches in this country.

But the Lucas factory, which makes these retardas, has had to restrict production because of the demands of the more profitable armaments departments of their factory.

Wars will cease . . .

The slogan 'Wars will cease when men refuse to fight' has attracted thousands to the pacifist philosophy of life. This is little more than a pious hope. Throughout history wars have been conducted by a very tiny minority. Today, even if less than one in a thousand were prepared to fight, mankind still could be annihilated by a nuclear war. Peace is not simply a matter for individual action: it requires a concerted effort by everyone who desires peace to enforce disarmament upon those who oppose it.

This brief review of the evolution of war suggests reforms to society that may help eradicate war. If no one could make money out of the sale and manufacture of weapons, this would help. If nations cooperated rather than competed in trade, there might be less international tension. It would further help if conflicts within societies were reduced so that internal pressures to maintain coercive forces were not so strong.

Some people believe that such changes to society are a guarantee of immediate peace. But mankind has a backlog of religious, racial and political prejudices, inherited from the past 5,000 years of conflict, that will take many generations to overcome.

Haole *is the Hawaiian word for 'white man'. In 1971, Catholic Action of Hawaii estimated that over 3,000 nuclear weapons were being stored on the island.*

Nevertheless the emasculation of organizations that have a vested interest in armaments and war would be an immensely positive step for peace, quite apart from the obvious social benefits for society.

Disarmament proposals

It can be argued that the military–industrial complex is a greater enemy of disarmament than all the misunderstandings which undoubtedly do exist between countries. Misunderstandings can be erased; fundamental support for armaments manufacture cannot. This was shown in 1955 when the Soviet Union accepted the West's proposals for disarmament in their entirety – only to find that these were then withdrawn. As a result, 'the hopeful atmosphere of that time was . . . destroyed'.* This episode is of crucial importance to an understanding of the obstacles to disarmament and is worth recalling in some detail.

On 10 May 1955 the Soviet Union laid proposals before the UN Disarmament Sub-Committee which, amongst other measures, provided for armed manpower ceilings of 1,500,000, major reductions in conventional armaments and an arrangement for the abolition of 75 per cent of the stocks of nuclear and other mass-destruction weapons. They agreed to an international control organ with staffs of inspectors having unimpeded access at all times to all objects of control. The completion of all these measures was to be followed by further reductions in armaments.

The French delegate's immediate response was that 'the whole thing looks too good to be true'. The British delegate, after consultation with the government, said he was glad that the Western 'policy of patience' had 'now achieved this welcome dividend, and that the Western proposals have now been largely, and in some cases, entirely, adopted by the Soviet Union and made into its own proposals'. After listing the points of agreement, he said 'we have made an advance that I never dreamed possible'.

The US delegate, after two days' discussion with the American government, said 'we have been gratified to find that the concepts we have put forward over a considerable length of time, and which we have repeated many times during this past two months, have been accepted in a large measure by the Soviet Union'.

After months of procrastination, on 6 September the American delegate dashed all hopes of agreement with: 'The United States

*Bertrand Russell, *Has Man a Future?*

does now place a reservation upon all of its pre-Geneva substantive positions taken in this Sub-Committee or in the Disarmament Commission or in the U N on these questions in relation to levels of armaments.' In other words all the proposals urged with vigour and persistence only three months before were withdrawn.

There is, in fact, no difficulty in devising disarmament agreements: the difficulty is to force governments to implement them. In present circumstances the military–industrial complex have far greater power and influence than the ordinary people. People of all countries want peace but are bemused and confused by propaganda. Yet Eisenhower saw that this situation cannot last: 'I think people want peace so much that one of these days governments had better get out of their way and let them have it.'

For people in Britain, the starting point must be the British government.

11. Britain's bomb

We have made a successful start. When the [nuclear] tests are completed, as they soon will be, we shall be in the same position as the United States or Soviet Russia. We shall have made and tested the massive weapons. It will be possible then to discuss on equal terms.

Harold Macmillan, 1957

Such were the illusions. The pace of the arms race has shattered Britain's dream of equality with the superpowers. Britain is now a medium-sized European power, unrepresented at SALT (the Strategic Arms Limitation Talks). Yet the delusions of past grandeur remain.

Relative to her economic strength (measured by Gross National Product – GNP), Britain spends substantially more on armaments than comparable European countries. Relative to area, there are more nuclear bases in Britain than anywhere else in the world. This hopeless attempt at nuclear prestige affects defence strategy, military spending, the economy, foreign policy and, less directly, many other aspects of society. It is strange that such a major issue receives little public attention.

The original decision to 'go nuclear' was taken by Prime Minister Clement Attlee in the late 1940s, on the recommendation of his military advisers, without informing even the British government. It was only years later that the public were told. Since then it has proved impossible to call a halt. Even though all the original arguments for a nuclear weapons programme – such as that quoted at the head of this chapter – have proved false, the policies of successive governments have not changed.

Until about 1965 we knew why. More recently the justification has been argued behind closed doors. This secrecy is said to be for 'security reasons' but, more likely, the government fears public debate. Their case is rarely explained and, if it is, often in terms that are dated and contradictory.

It is bizarre to recall that one of the pledges made by the Labour Party when it won the 1964 General Election was to abandon the so-called 'independent British nuclear deterrent'. The Party's Manifesto stated firmly: 'It will not be independent and it will not be British and it will not deter . . . We are not prepared to continue this endless duplication of nuclear weapons.' The essence of the 1964 pledge has been reaffirmed at subsequent Labour Party Conferences whilst the government, Labour or Conservative, has pursued the opposite policy. Indeed it was the 1964–70 Labour government that launched and blessed Britain's Polaris fleet.

Britain's nuclear status has an influence on the SALT negotiations and on the attitudes of near-nuclear countries. It is because of these international implications that the three elements of the so-called 'independent British nuclear deterrent' must be examined from the military and political standpoint although, ultimately, the possession of nuclear weapons is a moral issue.

Independent?

Nuclear weapons are supposed to give Britain the power to pursue independent initiatives in foreign affairs. However, non-nuclear countries such as Sweden, Austria and Algeria show far greater independence in practice. By contrast Britain has adhered totally to US foreign policy, especially over issues such as the Vietnam War, European security and the SALT negotiations.

This is not surprising since the so-called independent British nuclear deterrent was acquired as a result of a deal – the 1962 Nassau agreement – in which Britain obtained Polaris 'know-how' from the US in exchange for guarantees for US bases in Britain. These bases necessitate close Anglo–American coordination, as they link the two countries together in matters of peace and war. The price of the Nassau agreement has been for Britain to give America unswerving loyalty on all issues which might lead to their use.

British?

The military case for the British nuclear force is that America is unlikely to commit nuclear suicide for the sake of Britain alone. US Secretary of State, Christian Herter, made this clear: 'I cannot conceive of any President engaging in an all-out nuclear war unless we are in danger of all-out nuclear destruction ourselves.'

But who would Britain fight independently with nuclear weapons? Not America or Russia – either could annihilate Britain very quickly, and the four nuclear submarines (with only one certain to be on patrol at any one time) are not a credible second-strike force against the superpowers. Nor is it conceivable that Britain would use nuclear weapons against a non-nuclear power; if she did, America or Russia might well object. That leaves China, France and perhaps India as potential candidates for a British nuclear attack.

Common sense dictates that the British nuclear submarines are credible only as *part* of the NATO nuclear striking force. Rather than admit that Britain no longer has its own credible nuclear force, the myth that the missiles are British is maintained for political reasons. There are moreover suggestions that

America has retained an 'electronic key' which prevents 'British' SLBMs being fired without sanction from Washington.

Deterrent?

One thing is certain: if there is a nuclear war, Britain will be a target. East Anglia contains a greater density of nuclear bases than anywhere else in the world. The Clyde bases contain, or hold in transit, more nuclear destructive power than any other bases in Europe. These bases are said to add to our security by deterring our enemies.

It is equally likely that those bases will incite a nuclear attack. The more a potential enemy is convinced of their serious purpose, the more urgent will be his desire to eliminate the threat. Speaking in 1961, the British Foreign Secretary (later Prime Minister) Alec Douglas-Home emphasized this commitment: 'The British people are prepared if necessary to be blown to atomic dust.' Whereas countries such as Sweden and Austria may be spared from nuclear attack (though not the subsequent

'It is a matter of political, not moral judgment,'—Mr Denis Healey

fall-out), in the event of war Britain will be attacked quickly to eliminate her ability to retaliate.

Thus, because of the way Britain acquired her nuclear forces, these are neither independent, nor British, nor able to deter. The Polaris fleet is a waste of money for Britain, a powerful argument for France, China, India and other near-nuclear countries to join the nuclear club and a minor yet significant complication for the SALT negotiations. Many people who are resigned to the nuclear arms race between America and Russia do not see why Britain has also to be involved.

Morality

These arguments suggest that Britain's nuclear weapons do not make political or military sense. But nuclear weapons also raise moral questions. Are there *any* circumstances in which the use, or threatened use, of nuclear weapons can be justified?

A nuclear war would bring suffering and death to millions of people throughout the world. Most would be innocent of any crime – save, perhaps, acceptance of their own government's policies. A full-scale war would severely cripple or destroy the belligerent countries – and vast numbers of non-belligerents.

It is difficult to imagine a cause or provocation so great as to justify the unleashing of such destruction upon the human race. The destruction would be so great, so purposeless and so indiscriminate that – assuming the 'good' side won – it is hard to believe that the 'good' from the war would counter-balance such unprecedented evil.

Even some supporters of nuclear weapons accept that nuclear war is totally evil. They rationalize their support on the grounds that (our) nuclear weapons exist purely to prevent war. This debating point would be valid if it were certain that the (good) nuclear bombs will never be used. But, to deter effectively, armed forces must be ready and prepared for a nuclear attack. How could these forces be kept idle in a nuclear war? Moreover people who use this argument clearly believe that our nuclear weapons are intended *solely* for deterrence. In this case, how do they justify the development of MIRVs, SRAMs, ULMS and LRCMs as these *far exceed the requirements of deterrence*?

Naturally our present leaders are trustworthy, but can we be sure that America or Britain or the Soviet Union or some other country will not one day be led by a madman? Prime Minister Macmillan wrote to President Kennedy about nuclear weapons:

> If all this capacity for destruction is spread around the world in the hands of all kinds of different characters – dictators, reactionaries, revolutionaries, madmen – then sooner or later, and certainly I think by the end of this century, either by error or insanity, the great crime will be committed.

In short, British nuclear policies are *immoral* – because they contemplate the mass murder of civilians; *suicidal* – because they invite attack; *incredible* – because they offer no hope of victory; and *provocative* – because they fuel the nuclear arms race. They are also, and incidentally, very *expensive* and so largely responsible for Britain's excessive military spending.

Approximately three fifths of British research and development and nearly two thirds of all industrial research is financed from defence funds. Around two fifths of British R & D scientists and engineers are absorbed on defence projects. It is not so much the absolute value of this waste of resources that is important (though, at more than £5,500,000,000 per annum, this is serious enough). The misdirection of Britain's best brains on socially unproductive work has a profound significance far in excess of the monetary expenditure involved.

Britain is in a very special position. Unlike America or Russia she could renounce weapons of mass destruction without any loss of security and with great economic and political benefit. This action would be in the interests of Britain and of the world:

—There would be one less country able to start a nuclear war, fewer nuclear weapons around to start one accidentally, one

The dangers of leaving defence planning to 'experts'

Mary Kaldor, Fellow of the Institute for the Study of International Organization, at the University of Sussex

At a time when investment is declining, firms are collapsing and income is failing to rise, the defence sector is expanding as fast as ever. Military expenditures are rising in real terms and arms exports have exploded in size. If present trends continue, Britain could become one vast armaments factory, no longer a nation of shopkeepers but a nation of gun makers . . .

It seems to me that it is time we questioned this policy and asked whether the amount and kind of military expenditures which the 'experts' say we need is really so inviolable . . . The [military] situation is not as bleak as many might think. Nato spends substantially more on defence than the Warsaw Pact, and its superiority in active peacetime forces is 5,700,000 to 4,300,000. Even on the Central European front (always the scare ground in military thinking), Nato's position is not half bad. According to a recent Pentagon report, the slight Soviet superiority in manpower (now questioned) and in aircraft is offset by Nato's advantages in communication, infra-structure and the quality of equipment. The Great Russian Tank Threat is now much diminished since previous intelligence estimates apparently counted tank sheds, many of which were empty; in any case, Nato has an overwhelming advantage in anti-tank weapons which are the decisive factor in modern warfare. Finally, the Soviet naval build-up, which has agitated so many military journalists, is little more than an illusion. The Soviet Union has fewer ships than it had in 1958 – all that has changed is their deployment.

In fact, the counting game does not make much sense anyhow. That military balances are irrelevant in wars was surely demonstrated as long ago as the First World War. More recently the wars in Vietnam and the Middle East have shown that bigger and more 'sophisticated' weapons, on which the numbers game is based, can actually prove a hindrance in war . . .

Few people are aware that only 10 per cent of our defence budget is actually devoted to the defence of Britain. Surely something has gone wrong when a medium-rank offshore island, heavily dependent on borrowing to finance public expenditure and imports and badly in need of resources for new investment, spends so much money defending Europe, the Atlantic, and some distant dependent territories . . .

If wrong decisions are being taken, it is perhaps because they are left to the 'experts'. Defence debate is confined for the most part to a narrow community, representing the interested parties – the armed forces, the defence companies, or the research and development establishments . . . Information and ideas about defence need to come into the open.

(from *The Times*, October 1975)

less government to complicate negotiations for complete nuclear disarmament.

—It could encourage other people to press their governments to agree to disarm and discourage other governments who are thinking of acquiring nuclear arms

—It would enable Britain to take independent initiatives for world-wide agreement on disarmament and on action to overcome the problems of hunger and disease.

The irrelevant bomb

It is sometimes argued that Britain's bomb does not matter one way or the other. This is a change from the days when Prime Minister Alec Douglas-Home claimed that we needed the H-bomb 'to secure our place above the salt at the negotiating table' (nothing to do with the SALT negotiations – at which Britain is not represented despite the H-bomb!). At the 1960 Labour Party Conference John Horner of the Fire Brigades Union proposed the motion to 'cease unilaterally to manufacture and test nuclear weapons and . . . to prohibit the use of nuclear

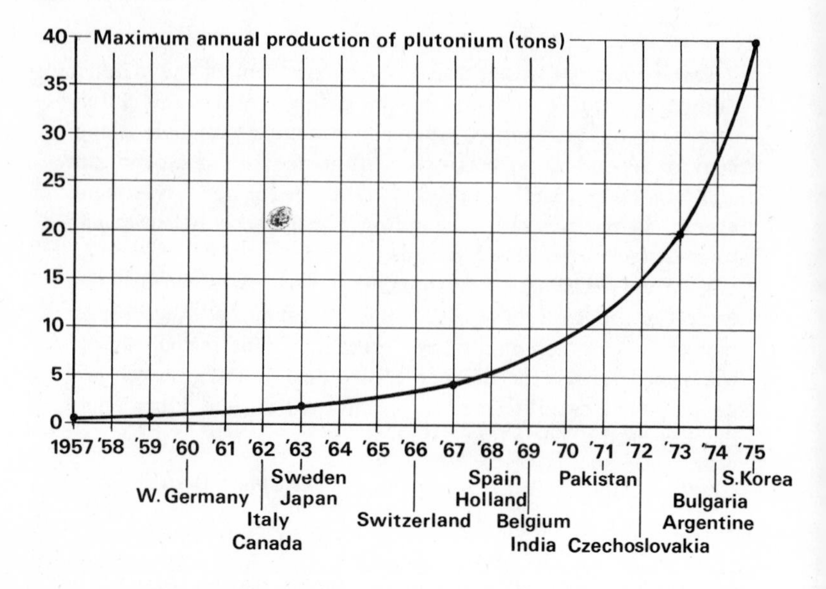

The increasing world-wide production of plutonium since 1957

Main events of the nuclear arms race

	1945	*1950*	*1955*	*1960*	*1965*
USA	A-bomb		H-bomb	IRBM	ICBM/SLBM
USSR		A-bomb	H-bomb	IRBM	
UK			A-bomb	H-bomb	SLBM (from USA)
France				A-bomb	
China					A-bomb
India					
Who next?					

weapons from British territory'. He pointed out that you cannot negotiate by saying: 'Failure to agree will result in my blowing my brains out.'

But, though largely irrelevant to the SALT negotiations, the British bomb is highly relevant to the issue of nuclear proliferation. In the same speech John Horner argued:

> It is said that three [nuclear powers] is better than four or five – I put it that two is better than three. But, if possession of the bomb has advantages for us, what right have we to declare to other nations that they should not also possess the advantage we claim for ourselves? . . . Indeed, if there is a single ounce of logic in the argument that somehow there is an advantage for Britain in having the bomb, we should be welcoming and not deploring extension of the Nuclear Club because everybody would deter everybody else.

When the Campaign for Nuclear Disarmament (CND) was founded in 1957, Britain was the junior member of a nuclear club of three. It was clearly unrealistic to expect either Russia or America to give up nuclear weapons unilaterally – that is, without a negotiated international disarmament agreement. But there was no pressing need for others to acquire nuclear

1970	*1975*	*1980*	*?*
MIRV	SRAM	ULMS	ASW/LRCM
ICBM/ SLBM	MIRV		ULMS?
		Euro-bomb?	LRCM?
H-bomb	SLBM		
H-bomb	ICBM		SLBM?
	A-bomb		H-bomb?
		A-bomb?	H-bomb?

weapons and, indeed, France resisted the urge for many years.

The nuclear race of the also-rans began when one extra country (Britain) joined the nuclear club. This made the French bomb well-nigh inevitable. China, the fifth of the 'Big Five' countries (with a permanent seat on the UN Security Council), was then in the anomalous position of being the only non-nuclear Big Power. Once China had the bomb, pressure grew within India to match the Chinese threat.

Britain has little influence on the main arms race between the superpowers but could still help prevent further nuclear proliferation. The most obvious step would be to leave the nuclear club, unilaterally if need be but, better still, in concert with the other minor nuclear powers. This would clear the air for the ending of the nuclear arms race through negotiation between the superpowers.

However, despite having signed the Non-Proliferation Treaty, Britain is not engaged in any negotiations for nuclear disarmament as required under Article VI. Worse still, Britain sells 'peaceful' nuclear reactor know-how and uranium to countries which have not signed the NPT. It seems that John Horner's suggestion in 1960 that Britain might welcome additional nuclear powers was remarkably near the truth.

Perhaps the greatest criticism that can be made of the nuclear arms race is its total irrelevance to the problems facing the world today.

By common consent . . . the basic problems of the human race in the contemporary scene are world poverty, overpopulation and pollution. It is this situation which lies at the root of the threat of world war, by design, accident or miscalculation, which hangs over mankind. Two thirds of the world's population suffer from undernourishment or sheer starvation. Of the 100 children born in developing countries every half minute, twenty die within a year and three quarters of those who survive suffer from malnutrition and have no access to modern medical care. It is estimated that 500 million people suffer each year from disabling diseases due to lack of clean water.*

*From *The Hungry Half*, Idris Cox.

The British used Christmas Island as a base for nuclear 'experiments' from 1956 till 1958

In the face of these facts people are remarkably quiescent. More is spent on armaments than on education – more in fact than the total production of all the developing countries put together. Why can't the developed industrialized countries cooperate to assist these countries?

The main reason is the serious political friction in the world which underlies the growth of nuclear armaments. If some advance could be made towards easing this tension, spending less on the deadly instruments of war, then far more resources could be channelled to assist economic growth in the developing countries.

Harold Wilson said, early in 1969,

> this is the only war we seek. The war against man's ancient enemies, poverty, hunger, illiteracy and preventable disease. A war we can fight the more successfully when improved world relationships, increased trust, enable us to turn from concentration on the munitions of defence to the munitions of economic and social advance.

These are fine words. Unfortunately there is little or no evidence of any serious endeavours by successive governments to end the 'concentration on the munitions of defence'. By taking resolute action for disarmament, and in particular by opting out of the nuclear arms race, Britain could lead the world towards peace and away from 'poverty, hunger, illiteracy and preventable disease'.

Book list

Hiroshima and Nagasaki

Hiroshima Diary, Michihiko Hachiya, Gollancz, 1955.

A powerful first-hand account by a Japanese doctor.

Hiroshima, John Hersey, Penguin, 1946; reissued as Penguin Modern Classic, 1972.

The experiences of six survivors. Hersey was sent to Hiroshima by the *New Yorker* magazine soon after the bomb was dropped.

Hiroshima: The Decision to Use the A-Bomb, Edwin Fogelman, Scribner's, 1964.

An examination of the political, moral and military implications.

Nagasaki: The Forgotten Bomb, F. W. Chinnock, Allen & Unwin, 1970.

A comprehensive account of the immediate circumstances of the Nagasaki bombing.

The H-Bomb

Brighter than a Thousand Suns, Robert Jungk, Gollancz and Hart-Davis, 1958; Penguin, 1964.

A classic (and very readable) account of the scientists' endeavours to understand nuclear energy and their reactions to the development of the H-bomb.

The Voyage of the Lucky Dragon, Ralph Lapp, Muller, 1957; Penguin, 1958.

The story of the Japanese fishermen who were showered with fall-out from the first successful FFF explosion at Bikini in 1954.

The Bombs of Palomares, Tad Szulc, Gollancz, 1967.

An account, by the *New York Times* Madrid correspondent, of how four American H-bombs fell accidentally on to Spanish soil.

Nuclear War

On the Beach, Nevil Shute, Heinemann, 1966; Pan, 1969.

The Chrysalids, John Wyndham, Michael Joseph, 1955; Penguin, 1969.

The scientific accuracy of these two novels is dubious, but they do convey the futility of nuclear war most effectively.

Effects of the possible use of nuclear weapons and the security and economic implications for states of the acquisition and further development of these weapons, United Nations booklet.

The best scientific appraisal.

The Arms Race and Military Strategy

From Yalta to Vietnam, David Horowitz, Penguin, 1969.

A good account of the Cold War for the beginner.

On Thermonuclear War, Herman Kahn, Princeton University Press, 1960.

Anyone who believes that no one would be mad enough to start a nuclear war should read this!

Arms Control, articles from *Scientific American* collated by Herbert York, W. H. Freeman, 1973.

An excellent compendium of articles on such topics as the history of the bomb, military strategy, arms control, etc. With good illustrations.

World Armaments and Disarmament, Stockholm International Peace Research Institute (available through MIT Press), yearly.

An expensive but invaluable yearbook giving up-to-date international information.

The Arms Trade with the Third World, Stockholm International Peace Research Institute, Penguin, 1975.

A reduced version of a report prepared by SIPRI.

Philosophy and Policy

Has Man a Future?, Bertrand Russell, Allen & Unwin, 1961; Penguin, 1970.

The Fearful Choice, Philip Toynbee, Gollancz, 1958.

This is a wide-ranging topic, and many books could be listed. But these two should make a good starting-point.

For schools

On the Warpath, John Cox, Oxford University Press (Standpoints series), 1976.

A sixty-four-page illustrated book on the subject of modern weapons and the arms race, intended to stimulate classroom discussion.

Films

The War Game (available from CND, Eastbourne House, Bullards Place, London E2 0PT; telephone 01-980 0937).

Commissioned by the BBC but never shown on television, this film simulates the effects of a nuclear attack on Britain.

Dr Strangelove (available from Columbia–Warner 16 mm. Library, 135 Wardour Street, London W1).

The famous full-length feature film.

A number of other relevant films are available from Concorde Films, Nacton, near Ipswich, Suffolk, IP10 0JZ (telephone Ipswich 76012). A catalogue of the films available is obtainable from that address, price 40p (post free), with a supplement of the most recent films, price 25p. The following films might be found especially interesting:

Energy: The Nuclear Alternative

Explores what fission power is and how it works.

Mr Nixon's Secret Legacy

Journalist John Pilger visits a Minuteman base in South Dakota and presents an awesome picture of the men and women working there.

Mururoa

The story of a small group of people who attempted to stop French H-bomb tests in the Pacific in 1973 by sailing into the test area.

The Palomares H-Bomb Incident

A Granada *World in Action* programme which examines the incident in more depth.

Glossary of terms

ABC *atomic, biological and chemical* weapons

ABM an *anti-ballistic missile* shoots nuclear warheads at oncoming missiles to prevent them landing on target

APW *anti-personnel weapons* are designed to cause suffering to people rather than destruction of military targets

ASW *anti-submarine warfare* involves all measures designed to locate, track and destroy hostile submarines

ballistic missile a missile that travels on 'free-fall' trajectory after its initial launch

CBW *chemical and biological weapons*

CEP *circular error probability* is a measure of the accuracy of a missile. It is the radius of a circle around the target into which half the 'shots' at the target can be expected to fall

counter-city strike retaliation against cities in response to a nuclear attack by the other side

counter-force strike a pre-emptive attack against military forces to prevent a nuclear attack by the other side

cruise missile a missile that can change its course either continuously or from time to time during flight

disarming strike another term for *counter-force strike,* employed to make it sound less aggressive

ecocide wanton destruction of the ecology of a country

first strike any attack which takes place without waiting for the other side

force loading numbers of nuclear warheads that are loaded on missiles, aircraft, etc., and can be delivered to targets in the enemy's territory

hard target usually a military target protected (hardened) by walls to withstand the blast overpressure (in pounds per square inch – psi) from explosions

ICBM an *intercontinental ballistic missile* (e.g. suitable for the USA/USSR range of around 8,000 miles)

IRBM an *intermediate-range ballistic missile* (e.g. suitable for the Europe/USSR range)

kill probability a measure (k) of the likelihood of a nuclear warhead with yield y (in megatons) and accuracy CEP (in nautical miles) destroying a target (ignores 'hardness')

kiloton the explosive equivalent of one thousand tons of TNT

lethality another term for *kill probability*

LRCM a *long-range cruise missile* is a cruise missile with the range of an ICBM

MAD *mutually assured destruction* means that each side in a conflict is capable of inflicting a level of damage equivalent to 'minimum deterrence' even when retaliating after a surprise attack

MARV *manoeuvrable re-entry vehicles* are re-entry vehicles like MIRV, but with the additional facility of being able to change course (manoeuvre) during flight

megaton the explosive equivalent of one million tons of TNT

minimum deterrence the ability to inflict an unacceptable level of destruction upon the enemy. This is commonly supposed to be equivalent to killing about a quarter of the population and destroying half the industry

MIRV *multiple independently-targeted re-entry vehicles* are sprayed from a single missile; each has its own guidance system and is programmed to aim at a pre-determined target

MRV *multiple re-entry vehicles* are sprayed from a single missile but, having no guidance system, scatter randomly

nuclear warheads these are carried by missiles or the re-entry vehicles (whether MRV, MIRV or MARV) of a missile and are equivalent to the nuclear bombs dropped from aircraft

NPT the *Non-Proliferation Treaty* (1968) provides for non-nuclear countries to remain non-nuclear and nuclear countries to work for nuclear disarmament

overkill the ability to destroy an enemy more than once

Polaris a nuclear submarine with sixteen SLBMs each of which, in 1975, had three MRV warheads of 200 kilotons and a range of 2,500 miles

Poseidon a nuclear submarine with sixteen SLBMs each of which, in 1975, had ten MIRV warheads of 50 kilotons and a range of 2,500 miles

pre-emptive strike another term for *counter-force strike*

PTBT the *Partial Test Ban Treaty* (1963) bans all nuclear tests above ground

SALT the *Strategic Arms Limitation Talks* between USA and USSR are intended to satisfy the obligations of the superpowers under the NPT

second strike retaliatory attack following a first strike

SLBM a *submarine-launched ballistic missile* – e.g. Polaris, Poseidon and Trident (USA), Sark and Serb (USSR)

soft target an unprotected military target (i.e., not hardened to withstand blast overpressure of 100 pounds per square inch) or a non-military target

SRAM a *short-range attack missile,* usually air-to-surface (i.e., launched from the air to attack targets on the ground)

strategic superiority more overkill than the other side

strategic weapons weapons for an all-out nuclear war (e.g., ICBMs, SLBMs)

tactical weapons weapons for a 'limited' nuclear war (generally with missile ranges of no more than 100 miles and warhead strengths below 50 kilotons)

ULMS an *underwater long-range missile system* using Trident submarines which may have twenty-four SLBMs per submarine with ten MIRVed warheads and a range of over 4,500 miles

yield the explosive strength of a nuclear bomb or warhead, usually measured in megatons

Index

Some Other Peacocks

A Bad Lot and other Stories *Brian Glanville*
Bird Count *Humphrey Dobinson*
The Blinder *Barry Hines*
Cobblers' Dream *Monica Dickens*
Conservation Scene *Geoffrey Young*
The Endless Steppe *Esther Hautzig*
First Love *Ivan Turgenev*
The Ghost on the Hill *John Gordon*
The Golden Ocean *Patrick O'Brian*
Help! *Barbara Paterson*
The House on the Brink *John Gordon*
I Can Jump Puddles *Alan Marshall*
King of the Barbareens *Janet Hitchman*
The Millstone *Margaret Drabble*
Nightfrights ed. *Peter Haining*
One More River *Lynne Reid Banks*
Ride a Wild Pony *James Aldridge*
Shane and other Stories *Jack Schaefer*
The Summer After the Funeral *Jane Gardam*
True Grit *Charles Portis*
Walkabout *James Vance Marshall*